POETIC DRAMA AS MIRROR OF THE WILL

POETIC DRAMA
AS MIRROR
OF THE WILL

by

MICHAEL BLACK

Wherein as in a mirror we perceive
The highest reaches of a human will
—Marlowe, *Tamburlaine*

VISION

Vision Press Limited
11–14 Stanhope Mews West
London SW7 5RD

ISBN 0 85478 074 2

For
Michael Tanner

© 1977 by Michael Black

Printed in Great Britain
by Clarke, Doble & Brendon Ltd,
Plymouth and London

MCMLXXVII

Contents

Preface

This book had its origin in a brief survey called 'Poetic Drama and Music Drama', contributed to *The Wagner Companion*, edited by P. G. Burbidge and Deryck Cooke. That chapter was meant to suggest a literary background to Wagner's dramas, in the sense that Wagner saw himself as the culminating point of a European dramatic art, not just a German musical art. So his forerunners were not solely Weber, Gluck, Beethoven and Mozart, but Shakespeare and Calderón, and ultimately the Greek tragedians. Thus Ludwig II of Bavaria could appropriately write to Wagner :

> My aim is to bring the Munich public into a more thoughtful and lofty state of mind by the production of serious and important works such as those of Shakespeare, Calderón, Goethe, Schiller, Beethoven, Mozart, Gluck, and Weber; to help it gradually to free itself from a taste for cheap and frivolous entertainment and so to prepare it for the marvels of your own works, facilitating an understanding of these by first putting before it the works of other great men . . .

This book pursues a modified argument in greater detail, exploring some of the analogies between the arts, and taking some care to preserve the distinctions between them which in the end make the analogies between poetry and music *only* analogies.

My knowledge of Spanish is slight, and it would have been prudent to say nothing about Spanish drama. But it is so often, now, passed over in silence in this kind of account, and is so important a part of the story, that I felt I had to attempt the brief note in chapter 7, and incidental remarks elsewhere. These are heavily indebted to the researches of Professor Henry Wells Sullivan of Chicago, which will eventually provide a standard account of Calderón's afterlife in criticism, scholarship and popular estimation. I am grateful to Professor Sullivan for discussing his work with me.

7

Similarly my remarks on the German romantic critics touch on a large topic which readers of English need now to become acquainted with again, in the way that they were before 1914. These passages are greatly indebted to Elinor Shaffer's important book *Kubla Khan and the Fall of Jerusalem*, and I have profited too from talking about her work with Dr Shaffer.

My views about Ibsen, which will seem derogatory and unsupported, derive from conversations with Ronald Gray, in which I tried at first to contest his well supported criticisms. The case is developed in his book *Ibsen: a dissenting view* to which I refer the interested reader, whose views may be either refined by the experience, or changed, as mine were.

Parts of chapters 3 and 4 were published in *The Melbourne Critical Review* and *New Universities Quarterly* and I am grateful for permission to use this material in modified form here.

I am aware that my use of the word 'will' at various places in the argument is an appropriation of the term for my own argument and, to the extent that it derives from Schopenhauer's more specialised sense, is a drastic reduction, corresponding perhaps to his 'intellectually enlightened will', the personal will of the single consciousness.

Cambridge   M.H.B.
February 1977

Introduction

I was tempted to call this book *Drama as Opera*. But the implied parallel with Professor Joseph Kerman's book (quite apart from the unlikelihood of matching his performance) will not hold. His title is justified : opera is indeed part of drama, and he shows why. The reverse proposition is not true : the rest of drama, what we have narrowly conceived as its whole, is not opera, nor part of it. Yet the temptation persists; many must have felt it, especially after reading Professor Kerman. It is worth developing the analogy a little here, though one is finally brought up against its limitations.

First, any comprehensive history of 'drama' would now have to take into account the relationship with opera—and indeed other forms like mime and ballet. They are part of drama, and to cut them off is to ignore part of the history : these forms had specific and important interactions with each other at given periods. Certain traditions underlie both drama and opera : the age-old tradition which became the Commedia dell'arte is a visible outcrop in both : perhaps in Shakespeare, certainly in Molière, Marivaux, Beaumarchais, Goldoni, Viennese popular theatre, English pantomime : equally in *opera buffa*. There would not be a comic nurse, sung by a man, in Monteverdi's *Poppaea*, if it were not for an old tradition of the comic stage. It would have been impossible to have had such a nurse in a serious opera a hundred years later, because French classical tragedy had supervened, and the old tradition was now thought vulgar and distasteful, and its survival an embarrassing and plebeian taste (when one wasn't actually laughing at it, that is).

At critical moments in the history of both drama and opera the two forms are in distinct relationships to each other. At the very beginning, the drama is dominant; towards the end of the seventeenth century the relationship changes; in the eighteenth century *opera seria* is a more vital form than neoclassical tragedy; in the late eighteenth and early nineteenth centuries a poetic drama tries to re-establish itself, and opera seems parasitic upon it (in the sense of being heavily dependent on it for plots), but in fact opera is already the more firmly established form, and throughout the nineteenth century is infinitely stronger than romantic drama. At the turn of the nineteenth and twentieth centuries, Ibsen's symbolic drama attempts a prose revival of hitherto poetic forms, and also attempts once more the deeply considered internal echoes and thematic development that Wagner had appropriated. It is a conventional judgement that Ibsen succeeded : a more critical judgement is that this wedding of Scribe and Wagner is largely a failure —was bound to be.

These borrowings, jealousies and rivalries between poetic drama and music drama are a continuous if fluctuating strand in the history of European drama. They depend on a genuine resemblance : both opera and poetic drama are attempting something which is higher than a prose or 'realistic' drama. They are both deeply conventional : they depend, for instance, on the understanding that a character will in his open verbal or vocal expression disclose himself more fully than people do in normal indifferent conversation. The expression of 'character' is therefore crucial to both. In the one case the medium of expression will be verse, in the other case the verse will be (should one say?) 'taken a stage further', and be sung. A possible analogy between verse and music is therefore established.

At a low level this analogy holds easily enough, and can be deployed through instances of the conventional utterances at their most stylised. For instance, you do not need to know Spanish (it is almost an advantage not to) to hear this passage as like a musical exchange. Two gallants approach each other from opposite sides of the stage, speaking antiphonally :

> *Federico:* Desta miseria guiado . . .
> *Enrique:*   Llamado destos acentos . . .
> *Federico:* Vengo a pesar del enojo . . .
> *Enrique:*   A pesar de la ira vuelvo . . .
> *Federico:* De madama, porque juzgo . . .
> *Enrique:*   De madama, porque pienso . . .
>   (*Mujer, Llora y Vencerás*)

It would be *better* sung. So would a good deal of Elizabethan drama in its duller patterned moments :

10

Queen Eliz: Ah, for my husband, for my dear Lord Edward!
Children: Ah, for our father, for our dear Lord Clarence!
Duchess: Alas for both, both mine, Edward and Clarence!
Queen: What stay had I but Edward? and he's gone.
Children: What stay had we but Clarence? and he's gone.
Duchess: What stays had I but they? and they are gone.

(Richard III)

There are other obvious musical devices—like echo scenes or oracular utterances or transformation scenes—in English and Spanish renaissance drama, and again one tends to feel that a fully musical setting would not be any less 'natural', but would get more expressive effect from what is essentially a matter of rhythm and melody in a mode which is not realistic and is all the better for being as far from realism as possible, therefore being sung.

The principal convention of poetic drama is the long speech or tirade, especially in the form of the soliloquy. From the very start, this was a main element of poetic drama: indeed one can say it developed faster than skill at handling dialogue. It was a prime interest, therefore, that a character should be heard delivering these considerable tracts of highly charged speech; and the audience took them, and developed a taste for them, as a virtuoso performance. The analogy with the dramatic monody of self-expression in music drama—what has come to be called in a general way the aria—this analogy presses itself upon us because the aim is closely related and one can develop parallels in each medium: also because there simply wouldn't be arias if there had not been soliloquies in drama.

So one is tempted to say that Shakespeare's verse is a direct counterpart to dramatic music—especially that kind of music which is concerned to carry the interchange or development of poetic motives in which the meaning of the drama might inhere, or the music which is directly expressive of character. It is an odd historical fact that the appreciation of, for instance, Wagnerian music drama has given us terms to reflect backwards in history, turning them on the analysis of Shakespearean or Racinian drama. So if we find in Shakespeare a richly motivic poetry, full of recurring themes, the whole tissue forming a symbolic system of internal cross-references, the temptation to equate verse and music is almost overpowering.

Nor should it be entirely resisted, simply because analogy is a useful tool and one can use it to explore a relationship where there are

11

admitted similarities. But in the end, verse is not music, and drama is not opera. One needs to preserve the identity of both forms : to see in particular what each can do that the other cannot.

This book is concerned with the nature of drama, and especially the poetic drama of England and France over the century from roughly 1580 to 1680. My main argument is that the achievement of this period is unique; it rises to its highest point in Shakespeare and Racine, and it is not exaggerated to say that the drama in Europe has never since risen to an equal height. The argument is somewhat technical in places, in that I am interested in the medium, the verse, and how it became the vehicle of deepest insight, and need to show this in detail. It will be seen that it did indeed set music a challenge, and we may infer that opera was in some degree a response to that challenge : dramatic music was offered as an equivalent to dramatic verse. The word 'equivalent' is used deliberately : I do not think or claim that music and verse do the same thing, and that one is therefore more successful or adequate than the other. It is true that they envisage the same objective : the expression—as direct as possible—of the movements of the 'will' (to appropriate Schopenhauer's phrase). But the 'will' does not necessarily express itself immediately in either words or music : it is very often internal, silent, non-verbal. Both words and music are in areas immediately adjacent to that central silence, so that expression may then come, as words, or music (or both) : but it may also come as bodily movement or dance or pictorial art or any other expressive form. It is therefore merely a partisan confusion of categories to say that Shakespeare's verse or Racine's is better than or not as good as Wagner's music. It is not foolish to ponder the extent to which they are doing related things.

The relationship does inhere, I believe, in the area that Schopenhauer suggested : in mediating a direct sense of contact with another centre of consciousness—a 'will', to go on using Schopenhauer's term, or a 'character' or 'self' as we more commonly say. It is the contention of this book that dramatic poetry does this uniquely well; it would also be my contention, if I were competent to argue it, that music *also* does it uniquely well. To argue that one is superior to the other is not only beyond my competence but, as I say, like comparing Rembrandt's self-portraits to Montaigne's Essays or Proust's *A la Recherche du Temps Perdu.*

12

Yet these temptations are strong. Who has not pondered the moment towards the end of Mozart's *Marriage of Figaro*? The original play, by Beaumarchais, gives us this (and little is lost in translation):

> *Count:* Here she is, coming out now. (*He seizes her by the arm*). Now gentlemen, what would be a just punishment for a hateful . . . (*Suzanne goes on her knees, her head lowered*). No, no! (*Figaro goes on his knees on the other side.* LOUDER) No, no! (*They all go on their knees except Brid'oison.* EXASPERATED) Not if there were a hundred of you! (*The countess comes out of the other summer house; goes on her knees*)
>
> *Countess:* At least let me be one of them.
>
> *Count* (*Looking at countess and Suzanne*): Ah, what do I see!
>
> *Brid'oison:* My word, it's my lady!
>
> *Count* (*Tries to raise countess to her feet*): Ah, so it was you, my lady. (*In a tone of supplication*) Only the most generous of pardons could . . .
>
> *Countess* (*laughing*): In my position, you would say No, No; but for the third time today, yes, I grant it without condition. (*gets up*)
>
> *Suzanne* (*gets up*): I too.
>
> *Marceline* (*gets up*): I too.
>
> *Figaro* (*gets up*): I too. There seems to be an echo here.

The patterned movement in that, the patterned sound, the neatness of symmetry go a long way. This is a comedy which knows how to pace things, how to place and move people, how to make a tableau, how to build a rhythm and milk a situation. And there is a perceptible emotion too: the Countess has a genuinely noble nature. But there is something more that can be done, to give depth. 'As for Da Ponte' says Professor Kerman,

> here is his contribution:
>
> *Count: Contessa perdono.*
> *Countess: Più docile io sono*
> *e dico di sì.*
> *All: Ah tutti contenti saremo così.*
>
> With this miserable material before him, Mozart built a revelation, and saw how it could be supported by other elements in Beaumarchais's scaffolding.

This understates the revelation itself, which builds up over a larger tract : from the moment where, in confusion, almost the whole cast is on its knees beseeching the count. This is economically rendered in the libretto as :

> *All: Perdono! ecc.*
> *Count: No, ecc.*

In the music drama it is a mounting exchange in which the beseeching for 'pardon' is twice answered by a straight high 'No' from the count (as in Beaumarchais), who then overflows into Mozart's own

> No, No, No, No, No, No !

in a stern descent like a steel ball going down marble steps. This wonderfully expresses his inflexibility, his triumph, his vindictiveness. At the bottom of this descent a woman's voice, as yet unrecognized, answers with an upward-curving phrase of some suavity and promise. This music, one can only say, in a very few notes, a phrase only, conveys an entirely different nature, and as the owner of the voice appears, she is seen through her disguise to be the countess. The count had seemed with his jagged descending figure to be closing or tearing something violently, or stamping : with her gentler upward run she has returned to the rhythms of an interchange between persons of quality. Five male voices recognize this with amazement, as the count and his supporters, Basilio, Bartolo, Curzio and Antonio, hushed, utter little astonished phrases :

> *Oh cielo, che veggo!*
> *Deliro! Vaneggio*
> *Che creder non so!*

The count now rises to the occasion, or more exactly kneels, and his beautifully full arching phrases express the other side of his nature, his genuine aristocracy of spirit. Convicted of being in the wrong by a much nobler nature, he has the grace to ask public pardon in a wholehearted way, and one warms to him at last :

> *Contessa perdono! perdono! perdono!*

Then comes the miracle Professor Kerman alludes to, when the Countess's last few equally simple words are given a musical expression, also simple in a sense, but of a beauty beyond description : the beauty being that of her nature.

14

The kind of direct intuition into her nature which the Countess's music gives is utterly unlike a description of her. It is actually one of the things which *cannot* be 'described' in words. It is often, in life, seen through words, but they are usually, as here, simple words which on the page lie inert. With people we know, we glimpse the personality, and love it or hate it : what we catch in the living voice, we catch also in the face. It is here that individuality resides, and our sense of an individual is such that we could not by the most laborious description capture it, if only because the description *is* laborious and indirect, and has to be turned by the listening mind into a carefully built-up set of responses. In the world the reception is immediate, felt not as words but as our whole sense of this person revealing himself or herself at their most characteristic. Equally, the face and the voice cannot be adequately described, for related reasons.

What we resort to, of course, is performance : an attempt to *be* that person to an audience who will see in that way what we are trying to convey. Mozart's phrase for the Countess is such that a good performance gives us a sense of this fictional personality almost as full and powerful, and more beautiful, than we often get in life.

I shall suggest that certain kinds of words, also in performance, are another mode of doing this.

It cannot be entirely fairly said that Da Ponte's words are 'miserable verbal material', since they so exactly fit the purpose—were just what Mozart chose to set to that music. It is indeed bare material; but it serves. The words are as basic an expression as can be imagined. They remind us for instance that in one play Shakespeare wrote the line

Never never never never never . . .

which could also hardly be simpler. In another he wrote

Die Die Die Die Die

which could hardly be more ridiculous. The words, either set to music or given resonance by a poetic context, give us access to some structure we are building up in our minds as we go along, a structure of inference about what is happening, its value and meaning.

It is commonly said that music, since it is not words, acts directly on us by avoiding an intervening conceptualization, and so might allow us to infer in the character depicted an inner state of mind which we intuit directly without the use of words. So it could, and we may even ignore the fact that words are being sung to this music. But there is another link between poetic drama and music drama: in life we are also always listening to words and inferring something which is not the words and is not only a 'nature', but is more like a process. We understand, we believe, what is going on in the other person's mind. He may think he is talking about indifferent matters or matters of fact. We receive a direct impression of him as a person nonetheless: this is mediated by the words, but this too is not the direct propositional content of the words. His choice of words, and his utterance or performance of them, are like a libretto and a score, in a small but real way, and it is our habit of interpreting those messages which gives us a start with opera.

It gives us a start with poetic drama too, where only words are used, but such words as no person actually utters in day-to-day converse. Our habits of speech interpretation help us also, more obviously, with dramatic poetry; but it is a medium which is not ordinary speech, as sung words are not ordinary speech. I go on to show (I hope) in the body of this book that poetic language is also an attempt to bypass some of the processes of conceptualization: to produce something more direct, like music. But that provokes an analogy, which remains only an analogy, however close. I come back to the proposition that music drama aims to do with words and music what poetic drama does with verbal music. It is the *objective* that is identical: to put us in contact, as direct as can be, with the movement of other minds, other wills.

This account starts in England and Spain in the 1570s. In 1576 the first public theatre in England was built in London. It was the regular stage of a theatrical company: a professional city theatre. It took (we presume) the well-known form of an open platform stage, with a canopy above, thrusting into a pit open to the sky and surrounded by tiers of spectators in galleries. It is often suggested that this was a natural development of the innyard.

At almost exactly the same time public theatres of strikingly similar general plan were being opened in Madrid. English and Spanish drama are alike in these respects: they are the products of the capital city, and promote some topics which are civic or national, or pertain in general ways to the prevailing religious and political

16

ethos. They both bring together audiences from every rank of society : they therefore appeal across the whole social range, to the 'community of consciousness' (Schelling's phrase). The dramatic forms which rapidly develop have an inevitable relationship with medieval drama, but it is the new element which is striking, and the rate of development is such that renaissance drama quickly establishes itself as much more new than old. In both England and Spain the drama is popular, conventional, national, and in verse.

Those four objectives are important for this study and deserve brief consideration here. 'Popular' can be negatively defined as the opposite of courtly or academic. This is not a drama which appeals to a restricted audience of the nobility, a superior caste, watching self-consciously as such. There are nobles in the audience, but as part of the whole social amalgam. It is not a drama, either, which is consciously learnéd, and is restricting itself by voluntary submission to externally decreed rules. It is more spontaneous than that, and as part of being 'popular' it aims to please an audience which has no externally applied criteria and is merely asking to be 'appealed to' (a better phrase than 'amused'). Directly appealed to, it directly responds; it will simply judge today's play, and yesterday's play is not used as a rigid measure. On the other hand, yesterday's play and the plays of earlier years on that same stage have produced a set of well-understood practical conventions, which the audience of experienced theatre-goers understands. These are conventions of staging and of the manners in which characters present themselves. They are remarkably free, and not in any modern sense 'realistic'. In particular, characters speak their thoughts aloud, and it is understood that other characters do not hear them. The other main convention is that the characters speak in verse. In Spain the verse-forms were numerous and intricate, and one assumes that the audience listened carefully and understood the transition from redondilla to tercet to estancia to octava to sonnet, and so on. These variations were meant to be expressive. On the other hand a medium which drew quite so much attention to its varieties and changes of mode is likely not to be transparent. English dramatic verse started as almost equally varied, but the final single mode, iambic blank verse, became transparent because it was the only mode, and so naturally close to the speaking voice that it was infinitely flexible.

'National' means that the theatre was a natural expression of the

17

community's self-consciousness. At a simple level this means that there could be plays on English or Spanish history, the sort of thing which contemporaneously might also go into a ballad, creating a spontaneous national feeling, which, once expressed, could be pondered. Less obviously, the theatre could treat themes which underlay social life at a deeper level. So there was a range of stimulus from simple jingoism to the kind of exploration of national myths found in the Greek drama (also popular, and more specifically religious than English drama, though not more so than the Spanish *auto*). 'National' also meant of the people as a whole, and speaking to them as a whole, so it is closely related to 'popular'. French drama of the late seventeenth century, for instance, is visibly passing towards the courtly, the academic, the regular. It does not have popular elements; it has ceased to deal with French national history. It is only national in the still quite important sense that it crystallizes the consciousness of the nobility and haute bourgeoisie who provided the statesmen, administrators, legislators and generals of a France rising to the apex of national political preeminence under the ancien régime. It was also national in a curious double sense : by proclaiming itself perfect, therefore fit for other nations to imitate, therefore international, it also secured French cultural supremacy by a happy self-deception. It remained highly conventional, but in a way where yesterday's play seriously limited the freedom or spontaneity of today's. But it too was in verse, of a kind which permitted a profound art.

The main argument of the first part of this book is that the highest achievement of the English drama and the highest achievement of the French have important affinities, despite the obvious differences. This can be put in a sentence : Shakespeare and Racine both produce an *internal* drama, a drama of the consciousness of the main characters, directly mediated to us by the verse. I go on to argue that this similarity was later obscured for historical and propagandist critical reasons. The eighteenth century became a kind of international battle between the partisans of a classical drama based on French practice, rigidly codified, and the growing number of adherents of a drama which tended increasingly to call itself 'romantic', but which was to be more specifically national, and which looked back to Shakespeare and Calderón as the giants of a pre-classical drama which was more spontaneous, more popular, more moving, less inhibited, and so on. It was still generally understood in the

18

eighteenth century that the highest form of drama was in verse. In the early nineteenth century the problem of language, though crucial, was not always seen to be so. It is arguable that just as the best regular or classical tragedies of the eighteenth century were in fact *opere serie*, so in the early nineteenth century supremacy in the drama passed to opera. Poetic drama was not convincingly revived, because the language used did not or could not provide the needed inwardness. In opera, even in the debased Grand Opera, the effect of music was to supply this deficiency.

2

Towards Shakespeare

Shakespearean drama is poetic: a great deal of the rest of Elizabethan drama is in verse. Inevitably, there is that difference. Many of the foot soldiers of that great literary movement were simply much smaller men, much smaller talents than Shakespeare, providing what they understood to be a marketable commodity, pleasing a public taste, and producing an article of no great quality.

It is necessary to keep the distinction in mind, or we fail adequately to value Shakespeare, or Jonson, or the best of Middleton, Tourneur, Chapman; and at their best these other men were poet-dramatists of a high order. But to make the distinction is not just a matter of dividing the vast output of plays into a small number of works of genius and a large body of mediocrity which can therefore be ignored or discarded. It remains genuinely a large popular literature, and writing the verse was a condition of rising to the poetry. The real taste that formed itself on Kyd and Marlowe was in some degree prepared for the enormous leap represented, surprisingly soon, by Shakespeare.

Both the poetry and the verse can be taken to start with Marlowe, whose plays have a strange energy because they combine intelligence and coarseness—are even in places what we are in danger of calling 'primitive'. In Act IV of *Doctor Faustus*, Faustus, troubled, sits down to sleep, saying:

> What art thou Faustus, but a man condemned to die?
> Thy fatal time draws to a final end;
> Despair doth drive distrust into my thoughts.
> Confound these passions with a quiet sleep.
> Tush, Christ did call the thief upon the cross.
> Then rest thee, Faustus, quiet in conceit.
> *Enter the Horse-courser, wet*
> *Horse-courser:* Oh what a cozening Doctor was this! I riding my

horse into the water, thinking some hidden mystery had been in the horse, I had nothing under me but a little straw, and had much ado to escape drowning . . .

(Faustus, like a music-hall entertainer, has sold the man a horse, saying 'Whatever you do, don't let him go into the water'. The courser thinks Faustus is meanly trying to keep him from some mysterious benefit, so goes straight off and does so. The horse turns into a bale of hay.)

> . . . Well, I'll go rouse him and make him give me my forty dollars again. Ho! Sirrah Doctor! you cozening scab! Master Doctor awake, and rise, and give me my money again, for your horse is turned to a bottle of hay! Master Doctor! (*He pulls off his leg*) Alas! I am undone! What shall I do? I have pulled off his leg!
> *Faustus:* Oh help, help! The villain hath murdered me!
> *Horse-courser:* Murder or not murder, now he has but one leg, I'll outrun him, and cast this leg into some ditch or other. (*Exit*)

A leg-pull, indeed: I suppose we get the expression from this kind of joke. The modern reader may be upset: this sort of thing won't do in high drama: how can the man pass from Christ on the cross to this buffoonery? Surely Marlowe didn't write this stuff, but some nameless collaborator: or if Marlowe wrote it he was cynically, or against his will, pandering to the common people in the pit, the penny stinkards who demanded (literally) horse-play. Or one says it's all just *primitive*: here we are at the rude beginnings of the national drama, and if they are as rude as this, the development is all the more remarkable.

Perhaps, though, we are now learning that being 'primitive', in a neutral sense, means not being like educated middle-class English-speakers of the twentieth century, locked in their cultural parochialism. It might mean being like the audience at a Greek play, or like the people who cast the Ife and Benin bronzes. That is to say, very sophisticated, actually: participants in an active culture which has its popular element and its high art, but does not keep them apart. Or if I reach for an analogy nearer our time, I think of Emmanuel Schikaneder, who was a comic actor in a similar popular vein and who was as happy as Mozart was to combine his comic business as Papageno with Mozart's music in *The Magic Flute*.

21

If you were to see this part of *Faustus* played by two actors of real gifts, they would make you pass effortlessly from the deep note of the verse to the comic business, and you would laugh, because they would *make* you laugh. On the page this kind of joke is tedious : it takes a comic actor of talent, or preferably genius, to make old routines come off. But old routines are old because comic actors can and do make them come off, and have done and will do for hundreds of years. The funny business of the commedia dell'arte was not written down for a good reason : it was mostly physical and all in the acting, but it included jokes like this. Let me slip in here that most of the humour in those of Molière's plays which are derived from the old traditions is of this kind. Honest students who doggedly read them in school and university ask why they are thought interesting, important, or even funny : they suspect a solemn literary fraud of an all-too-frequent kind—the dead classic. If they tried to act them, and if they had one or two comic talents among their group who would be physically inventive, acrobatically active, had a sense of timing, they would say the words as much with the body as with the lips. Energetically done, it would be a romp : well done, it would be more like a dance. Then they would see, and hear, and laugh, and be astonished, and see the point.

I introduce that note thus early partly because it is important, partly because it can only be pointed to and kept in mind. There is one enormous tradition in European theatre which can scarcely exist on paper : the great comic tradition of bodily humour which goes back as far as Greek comedy and beyond. One imagines it surviving the middle ages in wandering jugglers and tumblers and jesters. It becomes formalized, and given a set of synopses in the commedia dell'arte. From the commedia it is absorbed into some literary and musical high art : Shakespeare, Molière, Goldoni, Marivaux, Beaumarchais, Mozart, Rossini, Grillparzer, as well as in popular traditions : Viennese theatre, English pantomime.

But here in *Faustus* we have a routine. A magician, on a low estimation, is a man who performs magic, perhaps for profit. A horse-courser would expect a horse bought from a magician to do something remarkable. Faustus deflates the man's cunning hopes by making the trick a let-down, and when the man comes back blustering he plays another old trick on him. After the laughter, we are back with the problem that he has sold his soul to the Devil, and

22

time is running out. 'His artful sport', it is pointed out at the end of
the act, 'drives all sad thoughts away'. So he does not repent in
time, and goes to hell.

What was personal to Marlowe was a voice, which had a tone
and a movement like no other. There is every reason to think the
penny stinkards were struck by this music as much as they enjoyed
the comic business : in that they were like the rest of the audience
(except for those judicious persons who in all ages think the loud
laugh always speaks the vacant mind, or is as the crackling of thorns
under a pot). The music is like a jet which rises upwards in perceptible impulses, but only falls right back at quite long intervals; as
here :

> Nature that fram'd us of four elements
> Warring within our breasts for regiment
> Doth teach us all to have aspiring minds :
> Our souls, whose faculties can comprehend
> The wondrous architecture of the world
> And measure every wandering planet's course
> Still climbing after knowledge infinite
> And always moving as the restless spheres
> Wills us to wear ourselves and never rest
> Until we reach the ripest fruit of all
> That perfect bliss and sole felicity
> The sweet fruition of an earthly crown.

The unit is the line : if you look back at the passage from *Faustus*
you hear that each line is a unit of sense and sound. Here, however,
the lines are grouped. The first three lines form a sub-total of the
whole, and are spoken in one breath—if a long one. One then expects
a unit of comparable length, but the lines keep on pumping out,
each rising a semi-tone or so, until the highest note, at 'felicity' :
there is then a summating or explanatory flourish in the last line.
The speaker has made an exhausting point, in that his voice is acting
what it says; it is aspiring restlessly, line after line, moving as the
restless spheres, until indeed it reaches its goal, almost out of breath.
It takes a virtuoso to speak this, largely because the insistence, the
constant raising of the tone, threatens to go beyond one's vocal range
prematurely, and then remain a boring ostinato.

Indeed there are in *Tamburlaine* great periods of nearly twenty
lines at a time. One can imagine the thrill with which the original

23

audiences, transfixed, heard the actor's voice winding its way, mostly up and occasionally down, through these exhilarating passages, all expressing passionate vitality. For instance :

> What is beauty, saith my sufferings then?
> If all the pens that ever poets held
> Had fed the feeling of their master's thoughts,
> And every sweetness that inspired their hearts,
> Their minds and muses on admired themes :
> If all the heavenly quintessence they 'stil
> From their immortal flowers of poesy,
> Wherein as in a mirror we perceive
> The highest reaches of a human will :
> If these had made one poem's period
> And all combined in Beauty's worthiness,
> Yet should there hover in their restless heads,
> One thought, one grace, one wonder at the least
> Which into words no virtue can digest.

In his prologue to *Tamburlaine*, Marlowe advertises the special interest, the thrill, he is about to offer. He starts with what we call 'knocking copy' :

> From jigging veins of rhyming mother-wits
> And such conceits as clownage keeps in pay,

(so much for the competition. What of the clownage in *Faustus* and *The Jew of Malta*? Never mind that.)

> We'll lead you to the stately tent of war;
> Where you shall hear the Scythian Tamburlaine
> Threatening the world with high astounding terms . . .

The phrase is exact. The height and astonishment were genuinely new and produce a specific kind of drama—that of the supremely confident ego so sure of itself that it takes on the role of Scourge of God. Tamburlaine speaks straight out of the centre of that consciousness, and it is a kind of music that he utters.

But his is not a self-consciousness. It feels violent passions, within a small range, and they include a kind of stately love for his empress Zenocrate who is called 'divine' so that she may be the proper consort of a demigod in process. The concern for her produces another stately music which solves Marlowe's basic musical problem (how

24

to make long speeches when you are constantly raising the tone) by introducing a regular drop back to a refrain :

> Now walk the angels on the walls of heaven,
> As sentinels to warn th'immortal souls
> To entertain divine Zenocrate.
> Apollo, Cynthia, and the ceaseless lamps
> That gently looked upon this loathsome earth,
> Shine downwards now no more, but deck the heavens
> To entertain divine Zenocrate.
> The crystal springs whose taste illuminates
> Refinéd eyes with an eternal sight
> Like triéd silver runs through Paradise
> To entertain divine Zenocrate.

And so on : there is a good deal more. The musical sense here, as of strophes in a song, is created by a simple repetition at the end of a regular unit, and the romantic name at the end of the refrain gives it particular weight. It is a device used several times in *Tamburlaine*, and links with the more general habit of using names, especially exotic geographical names, to produce colour and harmonic richness.

The dying Tamburlaine has the hearse of Zenocrate brought before him for the last time. She had died long before, but he has carried the body about with him like a talisman, a reliquary, or even a trade-mark. He pours out his soul in a characteristic mixture of savagery and humanistic allusiveness :

> Now eyes, enjoy your latest benefit,
> And when my soul hath virtue of your sight,
> Pierce through the coffin and the sheet of gold,
> And glut your longings with a heaven of joy.
> So reign my son; scourge and control those slaves
> Guiding thy chariot with thy father's hand.
> As precious is the charge thou undertak'st
> As that which *Clymen's* brainsick son did guide,
> When wandering *Phoebe's* ivory cheeks were scorched
> And all the earth like *Aetna* breathing fire :
> Be warned by him then, learn with awful eye
> To sway a throne as dangerous as his :
> For if thy body thrive not full of thoughts
> As pure and fiery as *Phyteus'* beams,
> The nature of these proud rebelling jades

25

Will take occasion by the slenderest hair
And draw thee piecemeal like *Hippolytus*,
Through rocks more steep and sharp than Caspian cliffs.
The nature of thy chariot will not bear
A guide of baser temper than myself,
More than heav'ns coach, the pride of *Phaeton*.
Farewell my boys. My dearest friends, farewell;
My body feels, my soul doth weep to see
Your sweet desires deprived my company;
For Tamburlaine, the Scourge of God, must die.   [*Dies*]

That habit of saying 'now eyes', as if they were someone else's, or at any rate as if one wasn't right behind them, is peculiar to this drama, and especially to Marlowe. His main characters are always addressing themselves. Faustus's very first words are

Settle thy studies, Faustus, and begin
To sound the depth of that thou wilt profess . . .

The most common form of address to others begins 'Now [name]'; it is also a frequent prelude to a soliloquy:

Now Faustus, must thou needs be damned . . .

The habit of speaking to oneself as an *alter ego*, of haranguing oneself at times, is a specific stage in the development of drama. It shows an incipient self-consciousness, arrested at the stage where the self is not, in truth, very familiar with itself: not near to anything like a true self-knowledge.

Soliloquies in Marlowe are not very frequent: what looks like a soliloquy would be more accurately termed a tirade. The high astounding terms themselves inevitably ceased to astound an audience that grew in sophistication. The proof of that growth is parody. Since Marlowe was intelligent, one can imagine him in some moods laughing at the violent simplicity of what he was writing—even falling into the self-parody of sheer outrageousness (as in *The Jew of Malta*). The audience, for its own part, after a few years must have come to laugh (in some moods) at what is after all a very simple taste—but that does not prevent an audience in other moods (including a modern audience) thrilling to the same taste. But Shakespeare's Pistol (enshrined in many modern memories as acted by Robert Newton with much mad eye-rolling and mouth-twisting and solemn

26

gesture) was a devastating deflation of Marlowe's fustian, and must have been recognized as that :

Pistol: Shall pack-horses
And hollow pampered jades of Asia
Which cannot go but thirty mile a day
Compare with Caesars and with Cannibals
And Trojant Greeks? Nay, rather damn them with
King Cerberus, and let the welkin roar.
Shall we fall foul for toys?
Hostess: By my troth, captain, these are very bitter words . . .
Pistol: Die men like dogs! Give crowns like pins!
Have we not Hiren here?
Hostess: O' my word, captain, there's none such here. What the good year! do you think I would deny her? For God's sake be quiet.
Pistol: Then feed, be fat, my fair Calipolis.
Come, give 's some sack . . .
Give me some sack, and, sweetheart, lie thou there
                                   [*lays down his sword*]
Come we to full points here? And are etceteras nothings?

The way from Tamburlaine and Faustus to Shakespeare is via Marlowe's *Edward II*. This very fine and much more human play is anchored by the English history it recounts. Given the actual and quite specific events, Marlowe was faced with a different problem : showing them in a humanly convincing way. What we begin to see in *Edward II* is what we call character : each *dramatis persona* now has a more individual voice. We do not have a portentous phenomenon, like Tamburlaine, surrounded by ministering dwarfs and marching monotonously from victory to victory in very foreign parts. We have a set of actual English nobles engaged in struggle and intrigue, their fortunes fluctuating sharply, their actions springing directly from what they are. There is now very little rant : the speeches are short and entirely to the point.

The central character, Edward, progresses from homosexual playboy, frivolous, spoilt, but 'sensitive', to middle-aged martyr, genuinely pathetic. The counter-hero Mortimer evolves in the other direction from being one of a group of conspirators, and somewhat hotheaded, to a lonely dictator with a cold relish for power. This very progression was new : this is what we think of as 'character-development', and was an advance on the unchanging intensity of Tamburlaine. And both these characters see themselves in a dramatic light— 'present' themselves, so to speak. It is an important moment for the drama when characters become conscious of the role they are play- ing. Instantly another dimension is created : one is aware of these people not as mere centres of elemental power, as Tamburlaine is, but as centres of consciousness.

The effect is primarily on the music of the verse. It becomes flexible enough to accommodate different tones, therefore different voices. Mortimer has few soliloquies—only one of any length. He comes across as a sober calculator of deadly coldness :

> The prince I rule, the Queen do I command;
> And with a lowly congé to the ground
> The proudest lords salute me as I pass.
> I seal, I cancel, I do what I will.
> Feared am I more than loved. Let me be feared,
> And when I frown, make all the court look pale . . .
>
> They thrust upon me the Protectorship,
> And sue to me for that that I desire;
> While at the council table, grave enough,
> And not unlike a bashful puritan,
> First I complain of imbecility,
> Saying it is *onus quam gravissimum,*
> Till, being interrupted by my friends,
> *Suscepi* that *provinciam* as they term it—
> And, to conclude, I am Protector now . . .

The audible change from Tamburlaine's verse is in the level reflective tone; if the verse moves in a self-reinforcing way it is not now constantly jacking itself up. This is the steady note of control. We hear also much more frequent and natural pauses : a mind is working, moving this way and that; sometimes stopping. One mental consideration gives way to another, but they are all here giving satisfaction as they are surveyed. The last lines act a little scene : this is a consciousness which can feign, which can remember the amusing occasion and reenact it : can recreate its own false humility, can quote Latin not as a way of amazing the ignorant in the pit but as a way of claiming judiciousness. We are privy to all this as he speaks : he unveils to us a considerable complexity. And though in the soliloquy he is consciously displaying himself, he displays more to us than he does to himself. We judge him.

At the end of the play there is a sudden and quite unexpected twist : the successful schemer is defeated by the simpler people he thought he had under his control. With the same levelness he accepts defeat and death :

> Base fortune, now I see, that in thy wheel
> There is a point, to which when men aspire
> They tumble headlong down . . .

The verse here is supple enough to begin to do what it says : it rises characteristically, to 'aspire', and then tumbles into the next line,

> . . . That point I touched,
> And seeing there was no place to mount up higher,
> Why should I grieve at my declining fall?
> Farewell, fair Queen; weep not for Mortimer,
> That scorns the world, and as a traveller
> Goes to discover countries yet unknown.

Here is one of the first instances of that characteristic Elizabethan-Jacobean device, the 'philosophical' utterance by the doomed tragic hero. He moves downstage or turns to the audience. He is going to die : what words can he find?

This stage has no lights, but it is into a kind of moral spotlight that he moves. The actor is representing a man who is at this moment conscious of being in a dramatic situation—life has, as it were, responded to art, imitated it, and art is in turn a mirror of that life. The man is required to rise to the occasion, and preferably to master fate by showing himself untouched by mere mortal accident.

Mortimer here is characteristically sober and brief; his recognition of the fatality of his situation, and his simultaneous rising above that fatality is given in an image of some power. *Edward II* is full of premonitions of Shakespeare : this line probably gave Hamlet his 'bourn from which no traveller returns'—that is a typically negative inversion of Mortimer's positive setting out (and so tells us something about Hamlet's nature); it is more haunting and flexible in its rhythm than Marlowe's still rather stiff tramp; yet Marlowe has his own characteristic energy.

This drama swiftly went on to present scores of such self-dramatizations. They all produce the characteristic thrill of the proud ego stripped of everything but its pride, and always managing to find a superb rhetorical flight. It is not just a matter of rising to the occasion. This performance—and it is that—is a kind of self-validation, a reassertion of an ultimate personal strength. It is not inconsistent with seeing the pathos of one's situation—that is part of doing justice to it. But it is far from being inertly sorry for oneself, since that habit of talking to oneself by one's surname ('Now, Faustus') always indicated a kind of stance outside oneself, a way of seeing oneself as other. This distance produced two results : a lack of total inwardness, and this corresponding movement towards impersonality. The lack of inwardness means that the poetry is not that of the 'direct movement of the will' (to use again a phrase we must return to)—that it is therefore more rhetorical, more social, less personal. It produces suffering as a spectacle, which the sufferer himself half-approvingly surveys. If he can find adequate words, he comprehends it, in the full meaning of that word.

Here are some examples. Chapman provides several, notably the peroration of Bussy d'Ambois and Clermont of Ambois, his brother. Both are assassinated in renaissance intrigues of state so gratuitously violent that they verge on self-parody. Bussy dies to a music something like Marlowe's :

> O my heart is broken;
> Fate, nor these murderers, Monsieur, nor the Guise
> Have any glory in my death but this,
> This killing spectacle, this prodigy;
> My sun is turned to blood, in whose red beams
> Pindus and Ossa hid in drifts of snow,
> Laid on my heart and liver; from their veins
> Melt like two hungry torrents; eating rocks
> Into the ocean of all human life
> And make it bitter, only with my blood.

The text may be corrupt; even so, it is rant, of the kind Pistol loved —pretty ridiculous. Then the note changes to something deeper :

> O frail condition of strength, valour, virtue,
> In me like warning fire upon the top
> Of some steep beacon, on a steeper hill
> Made to express it : like a falling star
> Silently glanced, that like a thunderbolt
> Looked to have stuck and shook the firmament.

> [*Moritur*]

His more philosophical brother Clermont dies at greater length, and with greater subtlety :

> Guise, o my lord, how shall I cast from me
> The bands and coverts hindering me from thee?
> The garment or the cover of the mind
> The human soul is; of the soul the spirit
> The proper robe is; of the spirit the blood;
> And of the blood the body is the shroud.
> With that must I begin then to unclothe,
> And come at th'other. Now then as a ship,
> Touching at strange and far-removéd shores,
> Her men ashore go, for their several ends—
> Fresh water, victuals, precious stones and pearl—
> All yet intentive (when the master calls
> The ship to put off ready) to leave all
> Their greediest labours lest they there be left
> To thieves, or beasts, or be the country's slaves . . .

It is a long preparation, for a dying man, but it provides the well-laid base for a superb launching-off :

> So now my master calls, my ship, my venture
> All in one bottom put, all quite put off,
> Gone under sail, and I left negligent
> To all the horrors of the vicious time,
> The far-removed shores to all virtuous aims,
> None favouring goodness; none but he respecting
> Piety or manhood : shall I here survive
> Not cast me after him into the sea
> Rather than here live, ready every hour
> To feed thieves, beasts, and be the slave of power?
> I come, my lord, Clermont thy creature comes.
> [He kills himself]

It goes on just a little too long, beyond its own highest point ('Gone under sail, and I left negligent / To all the horrors of the vicious time . . .'). So does the death of Byron :

> And so farewell for ever. Never more
> Shall any hope of my revival see me.
> Such is the endless exile of dead men.
> Summer succeeds the spring; autumn the summer;
> The frosts of winter, the fall'n leaves of autumn :

> All these, and all fruits in them yearly fade,
> And every year return : but curséd man
> Shall never more renew his vanished face.

Wonderful stuff, in its way; but this too is followed by more, ending with

> Strike, strike, O strike; fly, fly, commanding soul,
> And on thy wings for this thy body's breath
> Bear the eternal victory of death.

Shakespeare with his cruel ear heard what was ridiculous in that, and duly took it off in *A Midsummer Night's Dream* (O die die die die die).

It was indeed a convention that was bound either to be laughed at or to be caught up in self-mockery. Flamineo in Webster's *White Devil* says, dying :

> My life was a black charnel. I have caught
> An everlasting cold; I have lost my voice
> Most irrecoverably . . .

and Ferdinand in *The Duchess of Malfi* :

> Give me some wet hay; I am broken-winded.
> I do account this world but a dog-kennel :
> I will vault credit and affect high pleasures
> Beyond death.

But his brother the Cardinal is wonderfully brief :

>   And now, I pray let me
> Be laid by, and never thought of.
>   *[Dies]*

Probably the best of all these effects comes from Middleton's *The Changeling*. It is one of the finest of the plays. It deals with a theme we think Shakespearean; a character is tempted to crime, succumbs, and then finds that the crime takes charge of her life, indeed changes her nature. She becomes 'the deed's creature'. She acquiesces in the change, becomes wholly evil, and comes to love the man who first served her purpose by committing murder, and then blackmailed her into bed with him. All its Jacobean trappings one accepts as the convention of the time; the moral truth of the play is permanent, and resides in the poetry. It leads to a couple of very much more real final speeches. To her father Beatrice says :

O come not near me, sir, I shall defile you!
I am that of your blood was taken from you
For your better health; look no more upon't
But cast it to the ground regardlessly,
Let the common sewer take it from distinction ...

Her accomplice De Flores takes the other line:

Yes, and her honour's prize
Was my reward; I thank life for nothing
But that pleasure; it was so sweet to me
That I have drunk up all, left none behind
For any man to pledge me ...

The convention here is splitting into two. Beatrice has reached a just estimate, and speaks from one kind of acceptance. De Flores speaks from another: he persists. So the drama tended to provide two views; that of a philosophical personage reconciled to fate and, if virtuous, rising above it because of his moral strength: and that of the bold bad man, who at the very end comes forward with a kind of glee, refusing to repent and going vigorously to Hell, where all the other interesting people will be. This is a continuing popular thrill: the persistence of Faustus or Don Juan legends in drama carries it forward in two moods. Faustus sins in a Promethean way, and cannot from a humanistic standpoint regret his science. Don Juan just enjoys his sins so enormously that it would be hypocritical in him to pretend otherwise. The pious spectator can thrill illicitly at the sight of all this very enviable misbehaviour, and collect himself at the end of the play and say 'serve him right'. In both cases the whiff of sulphur is a further thrill: actual devils taking the sinner off to punishment remind us of our own doubtful account with Heaven.

This brief anthology of dying speeches suggests a convention. Reading an unfamiliar Elizabethan tragedy, one turns to the end first, to see how the main characters face their death. Here is the high point of an afternoon in Elizabethan London: one can sense the hush as the doomed speaker comes forward. It is a vigorous popular taste, certainly, and a specially dramatic one. But we are arrested here at a certain stage in the discovery of the inner life.

So I should be surprised if readers unfamiliar with English sixteenth-century drama did not thrill to some of these passages. The effect is direct and strong; the verse is at least very accomplished and sometimes more than that; and the basic situation, where the doomed man is challenged to find words that fit his situation and show him to be able to rise above it, is in principle humanly interesting, indeed pathetic.

But then again I would be surprised if the reader seeing these examples all together, and knowing that there were very many more like them, did not think that the genre was in danger of becoming very conventional. An audience expecting a special kind of thrill was being given what it wanted. This is good Jacobean 'box-office', and rather too like certain kinds of aria in certain kinds of opera : too brilliant, or too lush.

So we face the critical problem of a popular genre which was also a commercial genre; and it is characteristic of our century to think that what is popular is bad. So it is, often enough. I am reminded of all those not very good films—no, *bad* films—that my generation sat through and enjoyed (knowing that we shouldn't) from the 1930s to the 1950s. Two things stand out in the comparison. In the first place, one can make the sober prophecy that long before four centuries are out, academics will be studying the popular film and being analytical about this art-form (or, alternatively, industry). The words which they will undoubtedly invoke once more are 'convention' and also 'theme'. What those who lived through the experience remember is that this was a process over the years, even an 'evolution', if the word may be permitted. Memory supplies some sadly trivial examples. The first time somebody said 'Stop ! I can explain everything !' we were greatly relieved; and when they said 'Why daddy, you're crying !' we were (I am afraid) touched. After a while the situations were seen to be repetitive and the responses formalized; we grasped (e.g.) that bad men wore black hats. A stage further, and these were old friends, to be greeted with a cheer, if not with ridicule. In the last stage, the art parodies itself. At the end of the epoch, one is left with a huge archive of commercial art, which lends itself very readily to analysis by convention. It would be wrong to say it is dead : indeed it still has a coarse life. Amongst it all, there is some distinctly talented work by people one is prepared to call masters of the forms, even if they did not make forms truly of their own. With luck, you may have one or two geniuses who go right through the walls of the convention.

34

I am not aware, alas, of any film-makers of Shakespearean genius, and my trivial examples do reflect something dishearteningly vacuous about the popular film, which cannot finally stand comparison with Elizabethan drama. 'Popular' turns out to be an ambiguous word. The Jacobean drama, on the other hand, produced Shakespeare, who both justifies and transcends the art form; Marlowe, who was a prodigy, and Jonson who was a very great artist. Middleton wrote one or two plays of very high quality, and Tourneur has great moments. That is enough to justify the Elizabethan theatre, even if the rest is, as Samuel Johnson said, easy, popular and therefore disgusting; and even if one or two men like Webster or Beaumont and Fletcher were skilled manipulators with a remarkable verbal gift, who felt no need to make their dramas self-consistent, still less plausible, and coasted along, like many a media-man today, giving the public what it wanted.

Yet I wish to claim that this drama is, in the mass, and not simply because it produced Shakespeare, interesting and important, and this because it was popular, conventional, and in verse.

'Popular' can now be given a more specific meaning than in my introduction. In the first place it means a real widely-shared taste, even if a 'bad' one. These plays touched a response in their audience of a kind which is not often seen in the theatre. For one thing it united the classes who composed the audience. There were some court plays, and Inns of Court plays, but generally this was not, I have suggested, a court-theatre, or an academic theatre : it was a city theatre and brought together the several 'estates' of London. It was also specifically English, and there are grounds for saying that its most important genre is not the much-considered but very limited tragedy of revenge, but rather the English chronicle or history play, which Shakespeare perfected, and the city comedy, which was free of his influence. The histories, from Marlowe's *Edward II* to Shakespeare's cycle, gave an English audience, gathered in London at the playhouse, or occasionally on tour in some county-town innyard, a sense of English history as vitalizing myth. The theatre was concerned to speak to its audiences in terms of their communal consciousness.

As proof that it was popular, it was speedily disapproved of. A permanent theatre can only be found in a city, for only a city can provide a regular audience. The theatre therefore only appears when there is settled city-life. But a playhouse creates a coming-together of all sorts of people, including prostitutes, pickpockets and confidence tricksters. A playhouse without artificial light can only function in the daylight—when people ought to be working—so it is a distraction from honest labour. Some people will get drunk and others will quarrel; some will make assignations with other people's wives. So there will be brawls and scandals. These are all reasons why the city fathers will disapprove of theatres and try to control them rigorously. More : some plays on English history will be understood to have current political applications. A cunning person may put on a certain play at a given moment, knowing that a popular audience will see the point of doing so : this will incite a riot. This happened, and to Shakespeare. That is one reason why central government will always suspect a living theatre and may seek to reduce its operation to a few licensed houses leased to safe people; one reason why it will censor plays.

The other reason is of course sexual-moral. The Spanish theatre had actresses when boys were still playing women's parts in England. Spanish plays specialized in travesty parts : women in breeches showed more of their legs than, in a Mediterranean country, was expected to be seen outside the bedroom of respectable married people : the parallel with the brothel must have been striking and altogether a great thrill. The Spanish theatre was also 'about' the point of honour, duelling, vengeance for injured chastity or marital rights. These were topics of immediate social concern, but also things to be treated soberly in sermons, not enacted in public. The English theatre was full of sexual intrigue, including adultery; it could be seen as a school of violence, fraud, and fornication, daring God out of heaven.

So the Spanish catholic puritans, like the English protestant puritans, hated the secular theatre. The reasons given for this hatred are plausible ostensible reasons, and the only ones puritans could openly press. The real reason, one may surmise, is simple : jealousy. A popular theatre is frequented with a joy not shown in a puritan church. But it is more than that : a popular theatre really is a centre of the community in a way which has real religious overtones. The consciousness of the community finds a genuine and spontaneous expression here, the numinous element of the community's history is celebrated : the national myths are reenacted, the nation's concerns are debated in the way that most involves the spectator.

36

It is a far cry from the dramatic festivals of Athens, but the Spanish and English theatres of this period were closer to the Greeks than anything we now have, and especially in this sense that the city-polity is manifesting a form of its corporate life—not consciously, but more truly for that reason. If you take into account the fact that Spanish drama evolved in the *auto* a religious form which gives an allegorical representation in honour of the eucharist, originally associated with the specific festival of Corpus Christi, the analogy with the religious element of Greek tragedy is closer than in England.

The second characterizing word for this drama was 'conventional'. I have already touched on one convention : that the hero facing ruin or death makes a speech, in which he cuts the rather fine figure of a man facing ruin or death and finding striking phrases, rhythms and tones in which to transcend his situation by stating it. At the least this is impressive rhetoric; at its best it is poetry; and at moments one comes to suspect self-parody or the tongue in Webster's cynical cheek. Other conventions identify themselves quickly and give no trouble. It is understood that a character may make an aside that we hear but the other characters do not; the final peroration is a special form of the soliloquy in which the character may unburden himself at length; and we gather that we are sharing his thoughts by a convention which allows him to speak them aloud.

There are extremely economical conventions of staging and time. If we are told that this is a forest, or a shore, or a cave, so it is. If we are told that years have passed, so they have. Nobody has any trouble with this initially : it is an enormous advantage to this theatre that a few props can be carried on stage, and we are off, without having a long interval for an elaborate scene-change.

One can imagine, then, a set of habitual theatre-goers in the London of the 1590s who by fifteen to twenty years' experience have mastered the conventions, so that the playwrights are free to use them without hesitation. Some of these conventions are so functional that they just disappear from consciousness, allowing the representation and the reception of the drama to proceed. Such are the conventions about place and time, and to some degree the soliloquy. Also, of course, the convention that people naturally speak to each other in iambic pentameters, though they may in familiar and coarse moments drop into prose. Here my second category, the 'conventional', subsumes the third, 'in verse'.

37

Except, of course, that it ought to be the other way round. The prime convention, the verse, makes the others operative. A character can say, for instance

> This castle hath a pleasant seat : the air
> Nimbly and sweetly recommends itself
> Unto our gentle senses.

Another character can reply to the effect that the presence of certain birds confirms the impression. What is happening here is that we are being told where we are—outside a castle—but in terms which do enormously more than that. A tonality is being established, and themes interwoven. At the same time the speakers are defining their natures. The first one is dignified, noble and trusting, willing to see good, and through his noble simplicity incapable of suspecting evil. Clearly the convention has taken a leap forward. We are not offered the equivalent of a board saying OUTSIDE MACBETH'S CASTLE. We are getting a segment of score, performed by voices which have a distinct personal character.

It was another convention that a character coming on stage could in a genuinely primitive theatre say who he is. When Faustus first enters and says 'Settle thy studies, Faustus . . .' his characteristic trick of self-address serves the humble purpose of telling the very simple hearer who it is that speaks. Shakespeare parodied this device in the mechanicals' play in *A Midsummer Night's Dream* and the pageant in *Love's Labour's Lost* ('I Pompey am, Pompey, surnamed the Big . . .'). The drama instantly passes the primitive point of simply representing that I the actor am this person (king or clown), and I do this thing (kill someone, fall down); that much could be done in dumb-show. The actor who speaks will say not only who but what he is; for instance :

> I am determinéd to prove a villain.

Ah, the audience may say, he is a villain. This is the convention that if a man says he is such and such, why then he is. But I am reminded of my not irrelevant comparison with the bad old film, where villains wore black hats. As soon as you reach such a point, you have to pass it. Either audiences get bored, or they send you up; the intelligent members will not indefinitely sit through mere variations of past experience.

38

Very much has been made by scholars of the conventionality of English renaissance drama. Indeed it is suggested that the conventions properly understood are virtually a key to the interpretation of all these plays. Some scholars will except Shakespeare, thus turning him into the solitary exception who proves the rule by transcending it. Others will claim that even Shakespeare is governed by convention : a perverse misunderstanding which at least has the merit of placing him in his time.

We do not however need to reject the description 'popular, national, conventional and in verse', which remains true. It is even true that at its very beginnings this drama is 'primitive', in the sense that the forms were not delivered into the world fully elaborated. What we need to grasp is the rapidity of the development, and by the end of that development the extraordinary flexibility of the conventions and especially the medium of the conventions, the verse. The central point of the scholarly argument, that everything is mediated *through the verse*, is true. One goes on to say that because the verse-form had by 1630 developed in the way (for instance) that instrumental music developed in the years 1780–1830, a 'language' was established which could express infinitely more than could be expressed in 1580.

Whether the audience 'demanded' that this should happen is hard to say. I think one could suppose that audiences would have fallen away, or would have changed their composition, if the process had not taken place. To reverse the proposition, the audiences which sat through this change became, by definition, the most sophisticated theatre-audience the world has seen. Or if that seems hyperbolical, the only comparisons that can be made with the London of 1600–1630 are the Athens of Euripides, the Madrid of Calderón, the Paris of Racine : the other comparisons would have to be musical.

The conventions therefore evolved, and their evolution is also the evolution of the verse-form by which they are mediated. The direction of the evolution is towards an internal drama, a drama of character, conveyed by a profoundly thematic structure where the themes are not just in some general sense symbolical, but represent directly the 'movement of the will'.

3

Shakespeare: from *Henry IV* to *Macbeth*

If you look back at the dying speech of Clermont d'Ambois (p. 31) you can see how much it is a literary product. That is, it has a structure, a procedure, which is rhetorical: the points succeed each other in a logically deduced way, and the rhythms are calculated: the whole effect is intended to be symmetrical and self-reinforcing; and it appeals to an audience assumed to be interested in effective ways of speaking—that is, public speaking as from a pulpit or in a court of law. It is persuasive oratory.

We have, then, the odd effect that at a supreme occasion for spontaneity—the unheralded moment when suddenly you find you are going to die—the dramatic character fortunately happens to have, in some metaphorical mental pocket, a well-considered and well-rehearsed speech, and comes out with it. We are impressed by the speech as oratory: once more a Jacobean hero has risen to the occasion and died, a rhetorician to the last breath.

A convention like that is bound to change, if only because intelligent audiences make the kind of reflection I have just made, and intelligent playwrights are in business to think of these things first. It was bound to happen that something more 'natural' was seen to be needed. The speeches by Beatrice and de Flores in *The Changeling* are more natural, because more in the character of the persons they have shown themselves to be. Even so, there is a rhetoric in their remarks, and something even more natural was still required. Not more 'naturalistic'; for 'naturalism' in its strictest sense would simply require that a stabbed man groans or shrieks or curses, and with a rapid loss of strength can at best mutter something brief, inaudible three feet away. We have had plenty of naturalism in the theatre— and in the cinema and television, where it can be better exploited.

Most of it tells us no more than we can learn by watching an accident.

What was required instead was another convention—which at key moments, crises, or for that matter at less important moments too, would allow important characters to convey the actual movements of a recognizable other mind, a character, a 'will' : more spontaneous in its movements, more fluid, more complex, more like the way the mind actually works. This would produce utterances much less like oratory, more like . . . and the only phrase that suits is 'dramatic poetry'. This essentially rises above the mere conversational small change in which we naturally converse, so everything would be formalized by the verse; yet the verse, becoming poetry, would be the instrument of a centre of consciousness discovering what it means to say and *all* it means to say only by managing to say it. This is the essential nature of dramatic poetry : that it is this direct access to an imagined consciousness. The words have the life, immediacy and force which simultaneously transfer a meaning and the sense of the spirit creating it. The character is not just enunciating propositions or even persuasive arguments : he is creating a sense of himself meaning to do those things but also giving us himself : and this self of his is felt with an intimacy that we do not often feel in life.

In Marlowe's *Edward II* the king's minion Gaveston, wanting to express his joy on being reunited with his monarch-lover, resorts to a figure of speech :

> Sweet Lord and King, your speech preventeth mine,
> Yet have I words left to express my joy :
> The shepherd nipped with biting winter's rage
> Frolicks not more to see the painted spring
> Than I do to behold your majesty.

As a piece of slightly mincing compliment it will do well enough. But we resort to the argument that it is 'in character' largely because we think it is a bit stilted; and there is still the sense that this poetry is paid out a line at a time. Listen now to another voice :

> O Westmoreland, thou art a summer bird
> Which ever in the haunch of winter sings
> The lifting up of day.

41

This is the weary king, Shakespeare's Henry IV, hearing, for once, good news. The jet of poetry issues and passes, as immediate as thought. It is borne on the rhythm and tone of a natural speaking voice, raised for a moment to something like the intensity of song. The flexibility of this voice (and its verse) is what strikes us. The same voice had earlier said this :

> Yea, there thou mak'st me sad, and mak'st me sin
> In envy that my Lord Northumberland
> Should be the father to so blest a son :
> A son who is the theme of honour's tongue,
> Amongst a grove the very straightest plant,
> Who is sweet Fortune's minion and her pride :
> Whilst I by looking on the praise of him
> See riot and dishonour stain the brow
> Of my young Harry.

Hear the earnestness with which the King turns to his interlocutor, taking him up, the forceful rhythm ('mak'st me sad, and mak'st me sin') driving over the line-end ('In envy, that my Lord . . .'), turning into the honest open-hearted envy itself, and then modulating into the painful comparison : all in one long varying period. The word-order, except for one line, is normal prose-word-order; the rhythms are those of energetic speech; yet the whole is magnificent dramatic verse : still, one must say, rather 'early', but evidently far beyond Marlowe's range. A master has arrived; turning the characteristically English form, the chronicle play on English history, into a work of fully achieved art. No apologies are needed for any aspect of these two superb plays, the two Parts of *Henry IV* : no-one can say they are 'primitive', or stagey, or boring.

This verse can do anything now : for instance that little gem of characterization, Hotspur, rebuked for his fiery outbursts, and bursting out in fiery reply :

> Why, look you, I am whipped and scourged with rods,
> Nettled, and stung with pismires, when I hear
> Of this vile politician, Bolingbroke.

(He stops short a moment. But he can't stop for long.)

> In Richard's time—what de'ye call the place?—
> A plague upon't, it is in Gloucestershire;
> 'Twas where the madcap duke his uncle kept

42

His uncle York—where I first bowed my knee
Unto this king of smiles, this Bolingbroke—
'Sblood! When you and he came back from Ravensburgh . . .
Northumberland: At Berkeley castle.
Hotspur: You say true.
  Why, what a candy deal of courtesy
  This fawning greyhound then did proffer me!
  'Look when his infant fortune came to age',
  And 'Gentle Harry Percy', and 'kind cousin':
  O, the devil take such cozeners! God forgive me!
  Good uncle, tell your tale—I have done.
Worcester: Nay, if you have not, to it again
  We will stay your leisure.

It acts itself: you can hear him snapping his fingers as he searches for the name, the exasperation at forgetting it compounding his other exasperation. And when he gets the name, he is off again, taking off the hated king, with his gift for cruel mimicry. Then a final expostulation, and he tumbles into a temporary silence. And then too, the other specifically Shakespearean touch: the 'candy deal of courtesy': the idea of licking something that melts, and that melting producing a wet mouth which is slobbering and nasty; this shifts instantly into the fawning greyhound, jumping up and licking you on face and hands, disgusting beast.

This is not the poetry of pen and ink, but the poetry of the mouth: a speech directly issuing from the movement of the mind, directly expressing the nature of the speaker, like Mozart's music for the Countess. It can present these sudden and startling images or analogies, but always in an earthy vernacular which is also given to folk-idiom, proverb and homely metaphor. The dying king speaks:

  Come hither Harry, sit thou by my bed,
  And hear, I think, the very latest counsel
  That ever I shall breathe.

With 'breathe' the dying man has reached the end of a breath and has to stop: the actor will take note of this and pause. The voice takes up again:

                      God knows, my son,
  By what by-paths and indirect crook't ways
  I met this crown, and I myself know well

> How troublesome it sate upon my head :
> To thee it shall descend with better quiet.

The 'by-paths and indirect crook't ways' are the natural metaphor :
they would not seem 'low' to a judicious educated hearer, nor would
they seem anything but natural to a peasant. But for a king to speak
in this idiom on the renaissance stage ! it is a remarkable thing, and
it was not to seem natural to critics in succeeding centuries. But the
naturalness is a condition of the greatness : in these words Henry
can speak his own mind : a mixture of painful conscience (for he has
been a ruthless schemer in his time; a successful Macbeth) mixed with
natural authority, and a sense that in the long run he is justified by
a reason of state to which he now actually and rationally assents
(though it also assists his conscience to do so). So he can feel real
scorn for the king he deposed and murdered, and this comes across
in the same vernacular comparisons as he goes back in his memory,
and warms to his theme :

> The skipping king, he ambled up and down
> With shallow jesters and rash bavin wits,
> Soon kindled and soon burnt . . .

(Bavin is firewood, or kindling; what could be more homely ?)

> Mingled his royalty with cap'ring fools,
> Had his great name profaned with their scorns,
> And gave his countenance, against his name,
> To laugh at gibing boys, and stand the push
> Of every beardless vain comparative, . . .

With recollection the scorn turns to anger; 'stand the push' becomes
an imagined contemptuous violence in the energetic puff of breath.
But I interrupt a magnificent onward sweep of scorn, which is both
self-justifying and justified :

> Grew a companion to the common streets,
> Enfeoffed himself to popularity,
> That being daily swallowed by men's eyes
> They surfeited with honey and began
> To loathe the taste of sweetness, whereof a little
> More than a little is by much too much.
> So when he had occasion to be seen
> He was but as the cuckoo is in June
> Heard, not regarded :

44

—again, a wonderfully direct, simple folk-comparison—

> seen, but with such eyes
> As, sick and blunted with community
> Afford no extraordinary gaze,

And here one sees that the curious phrase about being '*swallowed with men's eyes*' was not a mixed metaphor : it has recurred here in '*sick* and blunted'; it is something felt with the senses; and comes to a full-throated utterance at the end of the lines which complete the period :

> Such as is bent on sun-like majesty
> When it shines seldom in admiring eyes;
> But rather drowsed and hung their eyelids down
> Slept in his face, and rend'red such aspect
> As cloudy men use to their adversaries,
> Being with his presence *glutted*, *gorged*, and *full*.

> (My italics)

That is not just a magnificent long-drawn-out rhetorical utterance like Marlowe's. It has a life under the surface, where the images directly convey the complex shifts and associations of an individual mind, working strongly on an obsessional theme. For Henry sees standing before him a son who he fears is sent either to rebuke him or mock him or pay him out as a reborn Richard; whose gift of social ease and joy and easy living with common people is something that both shocks and allures him, and of which he is frightened, because it is irresponsible—but just possibly also jealous, because he is not like that but would secretly like to be. At any rate, his posture of being the sober, competent, politically adroit person who answered the nation's call and stepped in to save England from the irresponsible Richard is undermined when his own son shows evident pleasure in being *like* Richard.

We are inescapably in the area of 'character'. We only see a *dramatis persona* before us, an actor in his costume and role. We only hear his voice, and the voices of those he engages in conversation. But we are in following this interchange forced to ask 'why is he saying *that*?' The words themselves are not a flat announcement of news, nor do they just remind us of the past because the character is obliging the author by telling us what we need to know about events before the rise of the curtain. We are in any case at the end of a very competent play in two parts : it is simply too late to be giving an exposition. Nor is Shakespeare, at this stage in his career a tyro. Indeed his history plays, though they are not planned as a Wagnerian cycle, are meant to be seen as a succession and to be related to each other. What Henry IV now looks back on (as Wotan looks back in *Die Walküre*) is the substance of the play *Richard II*, seen by the victor as a much older, sadder man about to settle his account with God, the world, his kingdom, his son. What it tells us is the moral distance he has passed through since the first play : it tells us what kind of man he now is, as well as how he now sees the world. It is a different voice—deeper, more troubled; yet also firm in his ultimate self-assurance. What he has almost ceased to look for in his son is a transition, within a single man, from something like a Richard to something like a Henry, but self-redeemed and legitimate. The thing he has despaired of happens at the end of the play, and it releases Henry IV, so to speak, into history, and prepares us for *Henry V*.

We are infinitely beyond the primitive stages of the drama, and also beyond Marlowe's range of humanity. The drama now engages its audience at a subtler level. It does not cease to be popular, but it has ceased to be crude. It is still altogether conventional, but its conventions are supple and can be used to a wide range of effect. It is still essentially in verse, but a verse of a kind which will convey the deepest insights of Shakespeare.

Tamburlaine was a person to gape at : far beyond the experience of his audience, a mythical or world-historical scourge, not accountable in human terms. *Edward II* as a play produced a prototype Richard II and Henry IV. Shakespeare's *Richard III* portrayed the bold bad man in its double-dyed villain-hero. Yet it is noticeable that its opening soliloquy, in which Richard proclaims his aim—

> I am determinéd to prove a villain

—this speech occupies forty lines, and for a good many of them Richard is, without consciously intending to do so, explaining *why* he is going to be a villain. It is to get his own back on a world where beauty and straightness rebuke his ugliness and crookedness. His resentment springs from his hurt; but he will feel it as a cause of spite, and he will have his revenge. In other words, he is quite a complicated person, and an audience which just says 'he's a villain' because he is self-declared, is failing to hear all that he has said.

In fact no audience ever says just that, partly because of the hold that the bold bad man has on any popular audience (or sophisticated one, for that matter). Richard shows his devilish skill, charm, boldness, cruelty and so on in the complicated business of getting his own back on the world, and the audience loves to hate him (as the popular showbusiness phrase goes). There is no question of giving a boo, even a silent mental one, every time he appears : he fascinates.

The jump to Henry IV is very considerable, the jump to the related consciousnesses in Macbeth and Iago is greater still. When one asks where the difference of the achievement is localized, one cannot point to Shakespeare's mind or intentions, or to a reified tradition; one can only point to the black marks on the page—the verse. I now turn to Shakespeare's greatest achievements, and first to *Macbeth*.

> *Macbeth:* . . . Thou know'st that Banquo and his Fleance lives.
> *Lady Macbeth:* But in them nature's copy's not eterne.
> *Macbeth:* There's comfort yet, they are assailable.
>   Then be thou jocund : ere the bat hath flown
>   His cloistered flight, ere to black Hecate's summons
>   The shard-borne beetle with his drowsy hums
>   Hath rung night's yawning peel, there shall be done
>   A deed of dreadful note.
> *Lady Macbeth:* What's to be done?
> *Macbeth:* Be innocent of the knowledge, dearest chuck,
>   Till thou applaud the deed. Come, seeling night,
>   Scarf up the tender eye of pitiful day,
>   And with thy bloody and invisible hand
>   Cancel and tear to pieces that great bond
>   Which keeps me pale ! Light thickens, and the crow
>   Makes way to the rooky wood :
>   Good things of day begin to droop and drowse,
>   Whiles night's black agents to their preys do rouse . . .

That is 'evocative', everyone will agree. But it is not just a matter of atmosphere. This poetry is a tissue of thematic material : if you pluck a thread here, you will see a corresponding movement in the texture whole scenes away. Let me show this, first by saying what this piece 'means', and then by tracing some of the correspondences.

Macbeth is brooding uneasily; Duncan is dead and he is king, but he is not secure, and says why : Banquo and his son Fleance are a threat. Lady Macbeth in her over-easy confident way makes a little joke : she replies that as 'copyholders', their lease of life can be revoked, and also that though human nature is imaged or 'copied' in them, like all humans they can die and return to the mould. Her cynicism is that of self-assurance and strong will, which can make puns about killing people : an awful hubris.

Macbeth sees the point immediately : yes, they can be killed : he has just arranged that they shall. He is looking out into the evening light. He has plotted Banquo's and Fleance's murder for this night. He sees or imagines the bat and the beetle, and he evokes in one of them the squeaking haunter of churches and graveyards, in the other a call to a drugged sleep. 'Summons' and 'drowsy hum' and 'rung night's yawning peel' modulate threateningly into 'dreadful note'. It is a strange droning invocation, as if calling these powers to his aid.

Lady Macbeth pricks up her ears. But though he is now gloating, he enjoys not telling her. 'Chuck' is a chick, a little domestic bird : in his mind he distinguishes her from rooks, or owls, or ravens or birds of evil omen. He goes on looking out, and the verse moves from the slightly romantic if spooky note about the bat and the beetle to something very complex.

He is looking outwards at the setting sun, going down like a great bloodshot eye (compare the crude passage by Chapman, quoted on p. 30 for a similar image). It is looking at him, and he wants not to be looked at. So he continues his spell-binding by invoking the darkness that will hide it, and he thinks of night as a black scarf bandaging that wounded eye. But to 'seel' an eye is to sew the lids together (something done to hawks in training them) so the operation is a cruel one. 'Seeling' may get blood on the hand, and by an obvious homophony the hot red disc of wax waiting for the seal is suggested by the sun, and by the blood. Seals also suggest legal deeds, titles such as Banquo's 'copy', and he wants the bloody hand also to tear to pieces the deed which threatens him. If the eye of the sun is scarfed up, it will not see this happening, so the 'hand' (his hand), though bloody, will be invisible.

As the sun disappears, its great effusion of red light 'thickens', as shed blood congeals and darkens. The alliterative crow begins to beat

48

heavily through this thick medium, almost as if swimming, to the 'rooky wood'. One can only say that the 'k' sounds in some mysterious way thicken the verse sympathetically. The good things of day succumb to his spell : fall into a trance as if drugged (as Duncan's grooms were drugged before his murder); while the black agents (the crow, Macbeth himself) move into nocturnal activity. He, in particular, is 'rousing' to his prey, Banquo, but will not make this too clear to his consciousness and conscience.

This is great dramatic poetry : using the voice alone, it orchestrates the evil which Macbeth wills to support him and projects on to the world about him : it also follows the minute and astonishingly vivid associations of his inner consciousness at a level well below conceptual thought. But consider also the way in which the image-filaments stretch to quite distant tissues; or how the themes light up, and light each other up, through the play.

The most important correspondence is the idea of doing something, a crime, and wanting to do it, but being at the deep level so horrified by it that one wants not to be conscious of it, needs to be drugged or denatured. This is an essential moral element in the play : both Macbeth and Lady Macbeth think that if they can screw themselves up to it they can carry it off, that they will not be plagued by their own ultimate sensitivity. They are both wrong. This leads to interlocking chains of ideas. First, the scarf over the eye of day. This blinds, but the eye is already wounded by some violence, probably by the 'bloody and invisible hand'. Compare Lady Macbeth's earlier soliloquy : where she performs a parallel incantation, wills a similar violence to her own nature :

> The raven himself is hoarse
> That croaks the fatal entrance of Duncan
> Under my battlements . . . Come you spirits
> That tend on mortal thoughts; unsex me here,
> And fill me from the crown to the toe, top-full
> Of direst cruelty ! Make thick my blood,
> Stop up the access and passage to remorse
> That no compunctious visitings of nature
> Shake my fell purpose, nor keep peace between
> Th'effect and it ! Come to my woman's breasts,
> And take my milk for gall, you murdering ministers,
> Wherever in your sightless substances

You wait on nature's mischief ! Come, thick night,
And pall thee in the dunnest smoke of hell,
That my keen knife see not the wound it makes,
Nor heaven peep through the blanket of the dark
To cry 'Hold, hold!'

The raven, like the bat, the beetle, the crow, is one of 'night's black agents'. He is one of that flock of dire birds (the 'owl, the fatal bell-man', the 'obscure bird', choughs and 'maggot-pies' and so on) which culminate in the image of Macbeth himself as 'hell-kite' killing Lady Macduff and her 'chicks' in 'one fell swoop'. Here the blackness and hoarseness are thematic. The extraordinary invocation which follows, to unseen spirits, is a plea to be denatured in very specific ways. There is a direct association between 'unsex' and, for instance, 'passage to remorse'. The compunctious visitings of nature include a natural sexuality, love leading to fruitfulness. (We remember that the only good birds in the play are the 'temple-haunting martlets' on the castle walls. They are nature's visitors in the sense that they are 'guests of summer'; in and around their 'pendent beds and procreant' cradles they 'breed and haunt'.)

Lady Macbeth twice uses the word 'thick' here: of her blood, and of the night. A 'thick' blood is needed if it is not to be chilled by fear. The 'thick' night is like the 'thickened' light that Macbeth watches; in it things can be done but not seen—behind the scarf, or in this case under the blanket. The blanket is appropriate because a sleeping man, Duncan, may be stabbed through his covering. The wound is not seen, by heaven, or by the person who makes it. Yet she invokes, by denying it, the idea of a watching person crying out. One asks, is that not herself before being denatured?

Macbeth later has the same insight just before the murder:

Now o'er the one half-world
Nature seems dead, and wicked dreams abuse
The curtained sleep; witchcraft celebrates
Pale Hecate's offerings; and withered murder
Alarumed by his sentinel, the wolf,
Whose howl's his watch, thus with his stealthy pace,
With Tarquin's ravishing strides, towards his design
Moves like a ghost. Thou sure and firm-set earth,
Hear not my steps, which way they walk, for fear
Thy very stones prate of my whereabout . . .

50

This is the music of night's black agents and their magic again, the drowsy hum, the haunted tone of drugs and dreams : the self-hallucination, the necessary opiates. The 'curtained' sleep is related to the bandaged eye and the blanket of the dark which is going to be pierced. The most extraordinary sound here is the striding rhythm as Macbeth prowls, amazed at himself, across the stage towards Duncan's room, is horrified at the slight sound he is making and imagines it terribly amplified, giving him away. The 'stealthy pace' of the murderer is going in the end to turn into the 'petty pace' of the crowning soliloquy : it has the same remorseless beat, and in the end it tells against him.

The stage direction reads : 'A bell rings' : later, in her sleepwalking Lady Macbeth remembers : 'one, two : why, then, tis time to do it'. Macbeth converts it now into a knell for Duncan. (At the very end he thinks of clock time as a universal dead-march lighting 'fools the way to dusty death').

When he comes out after the murder, he has 'hangman's hands' : they are bloody, and not invisible. Hangmen, we remember, had to cut the victim down still alive, reach into him, disembowel him, throw the entrails into a fire, and quarter the body.

The 'good things of day' that had begun to droop and drowse had sunk into the 'curtained sleep' which was first abused by wicked dreams and then had the curtain pulled back by a murderer. So Duncan's sleep turns into that of death. Macbeth and Lady Macbeth themselves then enter into a prolonged and agonized inability to sleep naturally, which culminates in her sleepwalking scene. The sleeplessness is linked with the idea of bloody hands, which also become an obsession (after the shallowness of 'a little water clears us of this deed').

The 'sleeplessness' theme is introduced via the return of the 'accusing voice' theme :

> Methought I heard a voice cry 'Sleep no more !
> Macbeth does murder sleep.'

and this associates naturally with the 'bloody hands' theme :

> What hands are here ? ha ! they pluck out mine eyes !
> Will all great Neptune's ocean wash this blood
> Clean from my hand ? No, this my hand will rather

> The multitudinous seas incarnadine
> Making the green one red.

This is exactly paralleled later by Lady Macbeth's

> Yet who would have thought the old man to have so much
> blood in him . . . What, will these hands ne'er be clean? . . .
> Here's the smell of the blood still : all the perfumes of Arabia
> will not sweeten this little hand.

The most pervasive theme of all is blood : truly protean, as when the evening light is seen like blood, or the multitudinous seas are made 'one red'. Blood-images are therefore the link in important clusters. For instance

> I am in blood
> Stepped in so far, that, should I wade no more,
> Returning were as tedious as go o'er.

The notion of fording a shallow place on foot, and finding that it is not so shallow after all, and one may be caught by the tide and swept away by the 'multitudinous seas', links with that strange line in an early soliloquy

> But here upon this bank and shoal of time
> We'd jump the life to come

The bank and shoal is something you can rest on, becalmed, above the tide. 'The life to come' is something we don't trouble about. That may mean we shall cheerfully forfeit our chance of heaven so long as we reign secure here (as long as the tide doesn't come up); or it may just mean that the remaining part of life on earth is no threat, just a shallow current one can leap across. But the thing about banks and shoals is that the tide does rise, threatening to cut one off, and then one has to wade. So the tide of blood may become too deep to ford.

'Jumping' is itself a minor theme. In an early scene, when Malcolm is proclaimed heir and made Prince of Cumberland, Macbeth says, aside, in some dismay :

> The Prince of Cumberland ! That is a step
> On which I must fall down or else o'er-leap,
> For in my way it lies. Stars, hide your fires !
> Let not light see my black and deep desires :

> The eye wink at the hand; yet let that be
> Which the eye fears, when it is done, to see.

It is a little clump of themes. To return to the 'bank and shoal of time', the 'jump' is transformed at the end of that speech into this:

> Besides, this Duncan
> Hath borne his faculties so meek, hath been
> So clear in his great office, that his virtues
> Will plead like angels, trumpet-tongued, against
> The deep damnation of his taking off,

(The accusing voice theme)

> And pity, like a naked new-born babe

(another pervasive theme : the murdered babe)

> Striding the blast, or Heaven's cherubin, horsed
> Upon the sightless couriers of the air
> Shall blow the horrid deed in every eye

(the tender eye)

> That tears shall drown the wind. I have no spur
> To prick the sides of my intent, but only
> Vaulting ambition, which o'erleaps itself,
> And falls on th'other.

The sightless couriers are themselves the wind, and the murdered babe shifts into a rider of the winds; wind in the eyes makes them water involuntary tears, and can blow dust in them and make them sore. In an extraordinary metaphorical torrent, the weeping babe and cherubin ride upon the winds of heaven, invisible horses, which are going to drown in the tide of tears he has caused. As in a dream-shift, *he* is then on a horse, and is going to drown too. He has to spur the horse up, out of this tide, and all he has to do it with is his own ambition which is the horse he is on ('vaulting') yet is in a mysterious way, as in a nightmare, himself. The horse, defeated, falls back on the rider (the other) and this is also himself. It sounds like a muddled metaphor, but the 'muddle' is essential—it can convey the things he cannot present to himself clearly, and subtly reveals that the ambition is *him*, not some external force, and the conscience is also his. The vain leap is defeated by his own 'weaknesses', which properly exercised would be virtues. What he has crowding in upon him here as in a nightmare is a whirl of images passing into each other. The solid substratum under them all is his sense of the ultimately triumphant voice of murdered innocence, and in the face of that knowledge, his guilt, conveyed as a frantic immobility, clogged or self-frustrating. He and his wife are therefore like the 'two spent swimmers' mentioned in the very first scene 'that do cling together / And choke their art . . .'

The one passage from *Macbeth* that everybody knows is thought to begin 'Tomorrow, and tomorrow, and tomorrow', and is commonly accepted as a 'philosophical' statement—even as expressing a despair which is Shakespeare's own. That is a simple fallacy. To ignore the first two lines is to lose a vital part of the whole mental evolution, to ignore how the speech fits into the scene and the act : to ignore the way that it is dramatic. To take the words as Shakespeare's is also to lose what they tell us about the way Macbeth's mind works.

The whole act cuts between swift scenes : from the castle to the advancing troops outside, and back. Everything is moving to the final battle which will either destroy Macbeth or confirm him in his power. Within his castle, and within his sense of impregnability, he is at his most wound-up. There are significant parallel incidents. For instance, in V, iii he boasts

> The mind I sway by and the heart I bear
> Shall never sag with doubt nor shake with fear.

Instantly the servant enters, and his bragged-of composure explodes into

> The devil damn thee black, thou cream-faced loon !

and the following bluster. As the little incident passes, he moves into the deeper mood, the melancholy of

>   my way of life
> Is fall'n into the sere, the yellow leaf,
> And that which should accompany old age,
> As honour, love, obedience, troops of friends,
> I must not look to have ; but in their stead,
> Curses, not loud but deep, mouth-honour, breath,
> Which the poor heart would fain deny and dare not.

54

We are very close to him there; at any rate we feel the essential emptiness of his blighting achievement. But he pushes the thought away and moves back into the desperate energy, the brutality, of 'Send out more horses, skirr the country round, / Hang those that talk of fear . . .', the hectic ordering around of Seton, the distracted attention he gives to the doctor talking about his wife's mysterious illness. That is something he half-faces too ('Canst thou not minister to a mind diseased?') but when the doctor wisely confesses his power-lessness, Macbeth veers off into his mere energy ('Throw physic to the dogs, I'll none of it. / Come, put mine armour on . . .'). He even manages to deflect the thought of Lady Macbeth's illness into a grim joke: if the doctor can't cure *her* can he cure the country, can he purge the English away? He bustles off, leaving the doctor dry, dis-heartened and foreboding.

The action cuts very briefly to the advancing English, then back into the castle. Again Macbeth is at his frenetic morale-boosting—whether for himself or his hearers, who can say? Again there is a deflationary movement, but at first it is just a sound, a wail, offstage. Macbeth is checked, turned inward again, and in his 'sere and yellow leaf' mood reflects on his own insensibility. We, however, gather that he doesn't *want* to feel—can't afford to. It is a kind of prelude. Meanwhile Seton has gone off to discover what the noise was, and now re-enters. Macbeth comes back from his wearied side-glance at himself to ask, almost neutrally, certainly without premonition of what he is to hear, 'Wherefore was that cry?' There is, I suppose, a silence, and Seton then says, perhaps fearing an outburst like that poured out on the 'cream-faced loon', 'The Queen, my lord, is dead.' There is no outburst. There is, I think, another silence, as Macbeth struggles to represent this blow to his already deadened feelings. What, at this of all moments, is he to make of this of all disasters? He says an odd thing:

> She should have died hereafter;
> There would have been a time for such a word.

The tone is apparently calm, almost dry: superficially, the required stoicism. When you ask why should he say *that*? you see that there are contending underthoughts. One is a continuation of his previous thought: 'I am now past all feeling'. The other is more impatient:

'I am too preoccupied to have any spare attention for a thing like that'. It is also resentful: how *could* she go and die now? (We may remember the short story by Chekhov about the simple man who in the bitterness of his grief calls his wife a fool for dying.) At the bottom is the thought: I must get this battle over. If I lose, it doesn't matter what happens. If I win, there will be time to think of dying, or grieving.

But behind the mere shock, the preoccupation with keeping up a front, with facing the crucial coming event, if he had time to think it out he would see that he has lost the one person left to him with whom he might enjoy his victory (one point of the 'sere and yellow leaf' speech: he *knows* he has nobody else). The consciousness of this, a long way down, begins to seep through his resistance to it, and to well up in him like a wave of gall. So the rest of the speech follows. The 'time for such a word' is of course 'tomorrow', after the battle. He comes out with the word itself; and the bitterness of the thought that that tomorrow is now annulled as a possibility of any achievement brings home the pointlessness of everything for him, and he goes on, in a deadened ostinato:

> and tomorrow, and tomorrow,
> Creeps in this petty pace from day to day,
> To the last syllable of recorded time ...

On the surface this is not specially 'poetic'. It seems commonplace, even has something ranting about it, which comes from his bitterness, his emptiness, his self-inflation, and links with his violence. But it is not just rhetoric. 'There would have been a time' also had an undertone of terrible hopefulness or longing: he has spent the whole play trying to wade through or climb up, or jump or swim across to that point—to be home and dry on the 'bank or shoal of time', above the tide. It had all become focused on 'tomorrow', and now tomorrow is cancelled. It makes his past a hideous waste of time, and that repeated and twice stressed word 'time' unconsciously generates a rhythm and a set of images. The blank uninflected rhythm of 'tomorrow and tomorrow and tomorrow' has an obvious analogy with the 'tock-tock-tock' of a clock, and this generates 'petty pace'—the barely perceptible forward movement of the hand, which will go on until the 'last syllable' of the last clock, an endless meaningless march to a cosmic running-down. There is a pause. By a natural

56

antithesis 'tomorrow' reflects on 'yesterday'. And so he continues, in
the same dead clock-rhythm :

> And all our yesterdays have lighted fools
> The way to dusty death.

The fools would include Duncan, Banquo, Lady Macduff, her child,
the others. It is characteristic of his smallness and violence that he
thinks of his victims as 'fools'; but they now also include his wife,
and himself : they have been fooled most terribly. 'Lighted fools /
The way to dusty death' gives a momentary image of a funeral procession, a line of wavering shadow-figures projected on the walls of a
vault : so the rhythm has turned into a funeral march, quite naturally. Perhaps it is her grave, perhaps his : at any rate he doesn't want,
cannot afford, at this moment to look steadily at the phantasm; so
by another natural mental shift he moves on. 'Lighted' generates,
with the speed of thought, the idea of a specific source to be
quenched, so that the mocking shadow-figures it casts shall be
snuffed out. He breaks the rhythm with an energetic outburst : 'Out,
out, brief candle ! Life's but a walking shadow . . .'. The notion—of
puffing out at the candle an explosive breath—linked to something
itinerant, ephemeral, supposititious and distorted, equally naturally
shifts into the puffings of another shadow figure, who re-establishes
the treading rhythm :

> a poor player
> That struts and frets his hour upon the stage . . .

Here we naturally assume that he is coming close to a just estimate
of his own career. He has been a player in the sense of one who puts
on a borrowed robe, acts a part that is not naturally his (another
image-cluster or theme). He was also the self-intoxicated murderer
who moved over the stage with 'his stealthy pace, with Tarquin's
ravishing strides'. A 'poor' player is a bad actor, an unrewarded
actor, one for whom he, Macbeth, has a natural sympathy, but
nobody else has. 'And then is heard no more': the strolling actor
packs up his tawdry props and costumes and moves into a silence
like death. If he is a bad actor, nobody wants him back.

With a final awful transition, the procession of fools, the ranting
actor, shift into a madman, also stamping and puffing but unable
even to talk sense :

> it is a tale
> Told by an idiot, full of sound and fury,
> Signifying nothing.

The rhythm is suspended, and at that moment of ultimate bleakness, another messenger enters. Macbeth has passed in a dozen lines through a seismic experience, and come out on the other side into lucidity, even dryness: 'Thou com'st to use thy tongue: thy story quickly.' The messenger delivers a further blow: he has seen Birnam wood move. This time there is another explosion: 'Liar and slave!' But it is so brief that we see something has happened to knock most of the rant out of Macbeth. He ends the scene with his false certainties shaken, just wanting to get it all over with.

What we have seen here is not a philosophy, not even Macbeth's own 'point of view', but a dramatic process in which a consciousness undergoing a traumatic evolution is revealed through the words the character uses. We see and hear a crucial transition from false confidence to despair. Nothing is being said about the intellectual foundations of anyone else's world. What is transcendent about the passage is not the so-called pessimism, which is negligible as 'thought', but the way in which we are able to enter into this consciousness and follow its movements. The language takes us down below the level of logical transitions. The image-shifts, the verbal associations, the central rhythmic ictus and its transformations and suspensions seem the immediate activity of another mind, understood and felt as we do not ordinarily feel other minds.

4

'Will,' Self, Character

I have used more than once the phrase about catching or rendering the movements of the will. It comes ultimately from Schopenhauer, who claimed that it was the peculiar gift of music that it could do this directly. Words, because they use concepts, are necessarily in-direct and crude. Music is therefore the highest art—that was the conclusion that some nineteenth-century theorists reached, especially those influenced by Schopenhauer, and especially musicians or music critics.

As for the 'will' itself, it is a good word but needs defining in a general sense which will overlap with but also sharply reduce Scho-penhauer's more special sense. I mean here, as most people mean, the essential self, the individual human consciousness at the deepest level of its being. One difficulty is that as soon as one uses the words in this area one finds that they have both specialized and very general mean-ings, which are often in conflict. 'Will' is a word which can refer to various kinds of drive, some conscious, some unconscious. The will, the conscious ambition, to become managing director of a firm is not the same as the unconscious will that a dominant spouse exerts on a submissive one or a parent on a child. Neither is quite the same as the will in Schopenhauer's sense, which underlies both, and has to do with a total stance towards, or vision of, the world, which is both an expression and an internalization of the felt world, which is itself a working out of the universal will. Another word used to point in the same direction is 'self'. But many people who start out thinking that they are one self may at moments suspect or fear that they are several : a social self and a private self are frequent divisions. A word which has been used classically in France for the self is the 'moi'. This word is associated with our more modern 'ego', and it is some-thing people have come to suspect, together with 'self'. Egoism, self-regard, self-love, self-deception : these are the words by which a common kind of social wisdom touches on an area of deep difficulty, summarized in the fact that 'self-aware' people also know that awareness is always eluded or circumvented by the self, or the will, at its subtlest and deepest.

Introspectives and social moralists also point out a strange thing : that the self which performs these deceptions and asserts its will despite self-control is a universal self. It is virtually anonymous. The fact that its drives are so universal is one reason why such moralists posit a universal human nature : why the French moralists of the seventeenth century, working both from introspection and from observation of those about them, could couch their insights as universal generalizations unattached to any particular name : how people behave. Their generalizations are recognized as shrewd and true.

Yet it is also the case that these universal drives, like life itself, are only present in individual people, and always come out as personal traits of character. We cannot therefore predict behaviour entirely. We are in the habit of saying to people we know well, 'I knew you'd say that' or 'I knew you'd do that'. We can even say 'I know what you're going to say . . ." We cannot however on this basis predict our lives or others' lives, or the course of our relationships, because the individual personality is unique, and will always surprise us. We surprise ourselves.

The ego, the self, the will, as I have been touching on them are also related to the unfortunately named 'unconscious' or 'subconscious', which is more properly something of which we are partly conscious, but where the operations of the will, censoring or suppressing a full consciousness, distort or repress. It is also a matter of introspection that the operations of this will are so subtle, swift and multifarious that they operate faster than our self-inspection can bring them to consciousness, and that we often have no concepts for them. Hence, partly, Schopenhauer's intuition about music : since it doesn't use words it does not have to lumber along with syntax or be capable of conceptualization. Since it is not in words, the use of words to paraphrase it is especially clearly only a paraphrase and not a substitute for the experience.

All this is important for the drama in ways which it is useful to state. Let me start with a trivial example : a small scenario for a performance entirely in mime.

There is an imposing door, a closed one, in the centre of the scene. A young man enters, looking anxious. He approaches the door, stands before it, raises his hand to knock, then lowers it and walks away. We instantly infer a lack of courage. Now suppose that as he walks away he rather ostentatiously looks at his watch. We look at ours and see that it is five minutes to the hour. Suppose he comes back at the hour, knocks, and goes in. We then infer a quite complicated mental process, corresponding to the physical actions. His nervousness brought him early, and was such that it prevented him knocking. Since he knew he was early he decided that he didn't have to face the ordeal yet, so he put it off. Walking away, and imagining an observer who was inferring cowardice, he made a great show of looking at his watch, so that it would be understood that he was merely early.

Slightly odder : after an interval, the door opens, and the young man comes out. He is making a consciously dignified exit. But as soon as he is round the corner, he makes extraordinary faces, even performs extraordinary actions. Someone sees him and evidently thinks he is mad. He goes very red, and puts on a show of coughing, or suddenly wondering whether it's going to rain, or, once more, what the time is. We do not infer madness : we know that the strain of whatever it was that took place behind the door has now been completely removed, and that the internal psychic mechanisms actually demand some compensating activity of a purely physical sort : jumping, or waving the arms, or making meaningless utterances.

All that can be mimed, for a very good reason. Nothing has been said aloud—or for that matter internally. The young man has not said even to himself 'I am very nervous'; 'No, I can't knock'; 'I will pretend that it's simply because I am early'; 'I will now let off the internal pressures'. It is the normal condition of these states that any verbalization that takes place inside is 'sincere' ('Of course, I'm *far* too early'); but very little such verbalization does take place. One is simply knotted round the present crisis : intensely conscious of it, but not of oneself as observer, only as anguished participant.

Literature takes these matters as its basic material. Here are two examples from the novel, which has achieved its dominance as a literary form partly because of the possibility it gives the author of saying certain things direct to the reader. If my two little scenes were dramatized, the dramatist would run the risk that the audience would simply not see the point. The novelist can make it explicit.

David Copperfield is returning to Blundestone, home of the Peggotys, where he spent some of the few happy days of his childhood. What is he conscious of? Mostly of being more 'grown-up' now than he was then. But then this happens to him :

> A figure appeared in the distance before long, and I soon knew it to be Em'ly, who was a little creature still in stature, though she was grown. But when she drew nearer, and I saw her blue eyes looking bluer, and her dimpled face looking brighter, and her whole self prettier and gayer, a curious feeling came over me that made me pretend not to know her, and pass by as if I were looking at something a long way off. I have done such a thing since in later life, or I am mistaken.

The last sentence comes from the mature David Copperfield who is writing the book, but he does not now from his greater self-knowledge taxonomize, put into a simple verbal or psychological category, the experience which the child David actually felt as a sort of muscular contraction in the mind, a strange impulse of an unexpected kind.

Of course, these things can be put into words. Here is one of Stendhal's characters, Count Mosca in *La Chartreuse*, a mature self-conscious person, doing just that :

> . . . He returned to the Opera House and decided that it would be a good idea to hire a box high up in the third tier, from which he would look down without being observed by anybody, on the second tier boxes, in one of which he was hoping that the Countess would eventually appear . . .

She does, and

> . . . he rose to go down to the box in which he could see the Countess; but suddenly he felt almost as if he didn't want to call on her after all. 'But this is wonderful!' he exclaimed, and paused halfway down the staircase. 'I'm feeling shy! I haven't felt shy for a quarter of a century!'

'Feeling shy'—is that what David could be said to have felt? But Mosca's is a mature self-consciousness reaching for a ready-printed label, and with it covering up something more complex. The word 'shy' is not so much wrong as too limiting. It ranges the pure impulse of the psyche, what I called a 'muscular contraction' in the mind, with other things felt in the past by other people. We have to do that, but taxonomy always simplifies.

More important, the use of such labels gets us away from the direct experience into a merely verbal or conceptual domain, and we are tempted to be content with the substitute. You come to feel that David's state is adequately represented by the words 'feeling shy', and not by the preverbal impulse, the contraction. But the impulse has a direct link, not with other words, but with other impulses which may not be verbally linked. So we break up what is a mental continuum into discrete verbal counters, isolated from each other. If I suggest that 'feeling shy', as a mental impulse, is related to fear and to reverence, you will agree. But if I suggest it is also related, as a mental event, to envy, jealousy, dislike, you may be surprised.

My starting-point is that a very large part of our mental life consists in these preverbal impulses. In the nature of the case it is hard to find words for them, and one reaches for a metaphor. These things are like contractions, expansions, or brakings and accelerations. They are also pure perceptions of a complex kind : like passing someone in the street with a very striking or beautiful face. You receive it all together and at once; you could try to express it in several paragraphs of poetic prose, but that would be falsifying partly because it was so laborious about something that was itself instantaneous, and we know words are the wrong medium. A portrait-painter could do it : or Mozart finding music for the Countess's nobility. Think of being reminded of something you are embarrassed about. You don't 'think'; you shift in your seat and groan or wince. You don't say anything to yourself. Think of listening to music : one of the supreme examples of what I am talking about. You are preeminently *not* translating it into words as it goes along. If you were to translate it into something else it would be a language of gesture : hence, the dance.

We are here on a track which leads to much more important matters, which really do have to do with the will or the self at its deepest level. Take, for instance, this extended passage from George Eliot's *Daniel Deronda*, where we approach really important matters. You will notice at once that it is, in dramatic terms, a scene. A young man is on the stage, waiting. A door opens and a beautiful girl appears. There are indications of her costume, with its important colour, and what this does for her beauty. There are also the equivalent of stage directions for movement and gesture. There is a passage of dialogue. But consider what there is beside :

But when the door opened and she whose presence he was longing for entered, there came over him suddenly and mysteriously a state of tremor and distrust which he had never felt before. Miss Gwendolen, simple as she stood there, in her black silk, cut square about the round white pillar of her throat, a black band fastening her hair which streamed backward in smooth silky abundance, seemed more queenly than usual. Perhaps it was that there was none of the latent fun and tricksiness which had always pierced in her greeting of Rex. How much of this was due to her presentiment from what he had said yesterday that he was going to talk of love? How much from her desire to show regret about his accident? Something of both. But the wisdom of ages has hinted that there is a side of the bed which has a malign influence if you happen to get out on it; and this accident befalls some charming persons rather frequently. Perhaps it had befallen Gwendolen this morning. The hastening of her toilet, the way in which Bugle used the brush, the quality of the shilling serial mistakenly written for her amusement, the probabilities of the coming day, and, in short, social institutions generally, were all objectionable to her. It was not that she was out of temper, but that the world was not equal to the demands of her fine organism.

However it might be, Rex saw an awful majesty about her as she entered and put out her hand to him, without the least approach to a smile in eyes or mouth. The fun which had moved her in the evening had quite evaporated from the image of his accident, and the whole affair seemed stupid to her. But she said with perfect propriety, 'I hope you are not much hurt, Rex; I deserve that you should reproach me for your accident.'

'Not at all,' said Rex, *feeling the soul within him spreading itself like an attack of illness.* 'There is hardly any thing the matter with me. I am so glad you had the pleasure; I would willingly pay for it by a tumble, only I was sorry to break the horse's knees.'

Gwendolen walked to the hearth and stood looking at the fire in the most inconvenient way for conversation, so that he could only get a side view of her face.

'My father wants me to go to Southampton for the rest of the vacation,' said Rex, his baritone trembling a little.

'Southampton ! That's a stupid place to go to, isn't it?' said Gwendolen, chilly.

'It would be to me, because you would not be there.' Silence.

'Should you mind about me going away, Gwendolen?'

'Of course. Every one is of consequence in this dreary country,' said Gwendolen, curtly. *The perception that poor Rex wanted to be tender made her curl up and harden like a sea-anemone at the touch of a finger.*

'Are you angry with me, Gwendolen? Why do you treat me in this way all at once?' said Rex, flushing, and with more spirit in his voice, as if he too were capable of being angry.

Gwendolen looked round at him and smiled. 'Treat you? Nonsense! I am only rather cross. Why did you come so very early? You must expect to find tempers in dishabille.'

'Be as cross with me as you like only don't treat me with indifference,' said Rex, imploringly. 'All the happiness of my life depends on your loving me—if only a little—better than any one else.'

He tried to take her hand, but she hastily eluded his grasp and moved to the other end of the hearth, facing him.

'Pray don't make love to me! I hate it!' she looked at him fiercely.

Rex turned pale and was silent, but could not take his eyes off her, and the impetus was not yet exhausted that made hers dart death at him. Gwendolen herself could not have foreseen that she should feel in this way. It was all a sudden, new experience to her. The day before she had been quite aware that her cousin was in love with her; she did not mind how much, so that he said nothing about it; and if any one had asked her why she objected to love-making speeches, she would have said laughingly, 'Oh, I am tired of them all in the books.' But now the life of passion had begun negatively in her. She felt passionately averse to this volunteered love.

The novelist's contribution here is the direct comment, which not only explains what happens but says why. Some of this is a little heavy, with a remnant of the eighteenth-century confidentiality of Fielding, nudging us, and assuming a tiresome 'olympian' superiority to the characters. This is archaic, in George Eliot. But the sentences I have italicized are of an entirely different kind. The extraordinarily vivid image in the second, with its direct sexual connotation, puts us in touch with a movement of Gwendolen Harleth's self which is wordless, one of the contractions I have been talking about. But it is of very great significance; it is not just an incident in her daily mental weather : it is a clue to her entire nature, and ominous for her life as a whole. Only a metaphor will do, if this mental movement is to be conveyed as an experience rather than a concept.

One is tempted to say also that only a novelist can do that. But that is not true : the dramatist can do it too, by the same means, metaphor. He needs, however, a convention which enables his characters to say what is passing within them : to express themselves in a mode which uses metaphor in the same way. That it comes *from* them and expresses their inmost nature in a way which normal self-expression does not do makes it an 'unrealistic' convention, if one is using such terms. On the other hand we do not in life have God as novelist standing by either as narrator or as commentator. Any sense we have of what the moment means for others must come from our perceptions of what they say, how they move, how they look. The drama is in this sense always supremely realistic. We are left trying to make sense of it as we have to make sense of life, with the same clues.

I go back to my imagined paradigmatic evolution of drama (p. 38). Its first step is from 'I am a king', to 'I kill this enemy'. We have moved from grasping that this actor takes this role, to grasping that this actor performs this action in relation to another, and we recognize what has happened. That too can be done in mime : a man with a crown hits another with a wooden sword. But an actor speaking induces another dimension. If he addresses us in soliloquy, we say he is telling us about himself. If two actors speak, they are conversing. But both in soliloquy and dialogue, as we have seen, the basic convention almost immediately passes into something more complex. We ask 'Why is he telling us this about himself, and what does it tell us beyond his self-conception?' Or we ask 'Why, when *he* has just said *this*, does *she* say *that*?' In both cases we are going to infer an operation of the will, or the self.

I now link these considerations to what we have been seeing and hearing in the case of Macbeth. The notion of the will or self needs to be linked with the notion of character in drama, and both to the function of dramatic poetry. I wish to claim that the convention of Shakespearean dramatic verse, especially in soliloquy or aside, gives us an access to character which is unique in literature, and prompts comparisons with Schopenhauer's claim for music. The operations of Shakespearean poetry produce as verbalizations what is not in ordinary life entirely verbal because the ordinary person does not have the direct link between these mental movements and his capacity to verbalize, which is anyway limited. But the movements of the will may be rendered in words, as they may in music. Each way of rendering those movements will have its advantages. I cannot make, or compare, the claim for music, but I shall try to make that for poetry.

First I have to explain a historical difficulty about the concept 'character' and its use in discussions of Elizabethan drama. I have been developing an argument to the effect that English renaissance drama was highly conventional, and that the use of verse is the primary convention. I have argued briefly for an evolution in the use of the conventions—a fairly steady evolution towards a very flexible poetic medium which is peculiarly fitted to render the movements of consciousness because it is radically metaphorical, and therefore moves by a kind of mental-cinematic 'montage' from image to image. The limitation of the cinematic analogy is that it suggests something purely visual. Actually, nothing is purely visual: you only have to see an image for it to call up some other association which is not primarily visual, so even the silent cinema is not a purely visual medium. The procession of images which takes place in Elizabethan verse is very rich at its best, as I have been showing in the analysis of passages from *Macbeth*.

The consciousness which is mediated to us through these words is, we feel, an individual consciousness. The spectator has a distinct sense of the personality of Macbeth disclosing itself; and the more he sees and reads the play, the more distinct, therefore rich, that sense becomes.

But I have also been elaborating a sense of the motivic structure in the play *Macbeth*: showing that there are recurring themes, that these themes and their associations play right across the whole symphonic structure, and that the motives are, as it were, announced and developed by individual characters who are instruments in the play's orchestra. So they throw these motives to each other, and develop and return them, in an interplay which shows that no motive is entirely private to a particular character. The characters are therefore in a relationship to each other which is rather like that of members of a family, or instrumental group. The aim is not simply to explore one consciousness, or even several related ones : the play has a point beyond portraiture, and especially beyond the portraiture of the merely singular. These people are meant to be representative, so that we can't write them off as freaks, or cases. This drama has a social-moral aim : the people must serve as examples.

In literary studies we also have to remember once more that the novel comes between us and the drama. In the nineteenth century the novel became the dominant literary form : in one way it eclipsed the drama while opera was eclipsing it in the theatre. That is, we now read novels in preference to plays, and watch operas in preference to plays. The novel has carried the concept of 'character' further than drama could; because the drama is absolutely dependent on what the characters say, and nothing else; while, as I have shown, the novelist can intervene, directly or as disguised character, and can analyse and comment, providing a dimension the dramatist is denied. Plays have to be such that they can be played in a couple of hours : a novel can be infinitely long, and can follow a group of characters from cradle to grave, developing a relationship with them that the drama is denied.

Moreover, the English have had Dickens as great popular novelist. His theatre of grotesques has had an odd effect. The slump in Dickens's popularity in the second quarter of this century was due to the equations popular = bad, sentiment = sentimental, grotesque = vulgar, highly individuated = caricature, and so on. There was a reaction against that simple love of Dickens which took the form that he creates 'a world' of highly individuated people, lovable eccentrics or horrifying villains, all with simple recognizable features. You could treat these people as real, and you could release them, so to speak, from the covers of the book. They came swarming out into the general reader's consciousness, and you could play little games with them. (What would character X say in these circumstances? Since character X was recognizable by some verbal trademark, what he would say was always the same thing, actually.)

Admirers of the Art of the Novel—the tradition of conscious artistry since Flaubert—were disgusted at this confusion of orders of reality : for even the novel has its conventions, and with its capacity for a complex ordering of reality it is still no more 'real' than the drama. Both are black marks on paper—though the drama has the advantage of being performed and acquiring a dimension of reality

68

from the actors. There was in the 1920s and 1930s, and especially in the academic world of literary studies, a disgust with Dickens which rather rubbed off on the whole notion of character. It went side by side with those analytical—one might even say epistemological—enquiries into the status of the two arts which focused on their mechanisms and conventions.

The critical distaste for too much 'character' of the Dickensian kind joined hands with the scholarly analysis of the history of the drama itself which insisted on 'convention'. 'Character' dropped further into the background because of the reaction against the Shakespearean criticism of A. C. Bradley, who in the immediate aftermath of Dickens had looked at Shakespeare's characters as if they were real people, and had the same tendency to give them an extended life outside the drama. What had Hamlet studied at Wittenberg; how old was he, exactly, and where was he at the time of his father's death; how old was Macbeth?

Bradley's book, *Shakespearean Tragedy*, is full of fine criticisms of detail, where he followed the drama as drama. But he consistently develops this notion of character-beyond-the-play. He suggests, for instance, that it was very unfortunate for Hamlet that the action of the play took place when it did, since he was off-form. Had it been any other time, he would have managed to cope better. His behaviour would have been more in consonance with the noble nature we know him to have. We hear a good deal about what Hamlet 'must normally have been'. We learn this by 'reconstructing from the Hamlet of the play', and we get a 'Hamlet of earlier days', who was of course ever so nice.

This is simply illegitimate, and one inevitable reaction was to concentrate on the convention of the play. We have only these words, and the possibility of performing them meaningfully. There is nothing else: in particular no real person with a life outside the play. This was put analytically by the scarcely remembered but deeply influential critic C. H. Rickword in *The Calendar of Modern Letters* (1925–27)

> . . . the actual story of a novel eludes the epitomist as completely as character; few great works are not ridiculous in synopsis. And for this reason—that the form of the novel only exists as a balance of response on the part of the reader. Hence schematic plot is a construction of the reader's that corresponds to an aspect of that

69

response and stands in merely diagrammatic relation to the source. Only as precipitates from the memory are plot or character tangible; yet only in solution have either any emotive valency. The composition of this metaphorical fluid is a technical matter. The technique of the novel is just as symphonic as the technique of the drama, and as dependent, up to a point, on the dynamic devices of articulation and control of narrative tempo. But, though dependent, it is as dependent as legs are on muscles, for the *how* but not the *why* of movement . . . The organic is the province of criticism. More important, then, than what may be called the tricks of narrative is the status of plot and its relation to the other elements of a novel, particularly its relation to character in solution.

Already the drama is being treated here as poor relation or crude predecessor of the novel. Rickword can go on to say, as something likely to be agreed to by the sophisticated :

Henry James is often given credit for having been the first to assert that events within the mind might be just as important as those without. The claim is hardly just, but he certainly was the first to realize that the interior drama might be rendered immediately by language without the intervention of circumstantiating physical action at every stage, that the word was as capable of embodying mental as physical movements, and that its latter function was useful only because of its superior vividness.

Extraordinary! It was Shakespeare who did that, centuries before James. How could it be forgotten? Only in an age which despised the drama, or was being scholarly at its expense.

The historians of the Elizabethan theatre tended to postulate a drama in which the conventions were always given their original face value, in which there was no evolution. This too tended to militate against a fruitful notion of character : reducing it to a simple playing-card notion, where the character had the status that his convention gave him. So inner complexity was denied—still more the notion of development.

This historical model of the extremely convention-ridden form was linked in less historically oriented critics to Wilson Knight's concept of the play as 'expanded metaphor' in his influential book *The Wheel of Fire*. The play is conceived as an elaborately laid-out system or symphonic structure. The themes are dominant, and they subserve

70

a total vision which it is Shakespeare's intention to convey. The individual characters are entirely subservient to this overall purpose, and indeed become mere instruments in the orchestra again. They have no substantial human reality : in fact they are flat elements in an allegory.

Two powerful presences can be sensed in the background. One may wonder whether Wilson Knight would have used the musical analogy as much as he did, but for the example of Wagner himself. It was Wagner, after all, who turned the stream of symphonic music into the dried river-bed of one form of the drama, and his great structures do offer the analogy of an enormous system in which the individual characters play a specific part. The kind of thematic analysis which has been practised on Wagner (and which he invited, since the themes are undoubtedly there) has, I think, tended to reduce the individuality and interest of Wagner's own characters, and, transferred, would do the same for Shakespeare's.

The other presence is D. H. Lawrence, who since his death has had an increasing influence on various kinds of literary criticism. He produced a crucial utterance on character, much repeated in many contexts; not much understood, and potentially stultifying. It comes from the letter to Edward Garnett of 5 June 1914 :

> You mustn't look in my novel for the old stable ego of the character. There is another ego, according to whose action the individual is unrecognizable and passes through, as it were, allotropic states which it needs a deeper sense than any we've been used to exercise, to discover are states of the same radically unchanged element. (Like as diamond and coal are the same pure single element of carbon. The ordinary novel would trace the history of the diamond —but I say 'Diamond, what! this is carbon.' And my diamond might be coal or soot, and my theme is carbon.)

Well, where was the 'old stable ego of the character' to be found? I suspect in Dickens's grotesques again, and in the sub-Dickensian novels of Wells and Arnold Bennett, who deal in character of a determinate, individualized, finished nature. The characters they deal with are 'characters' in quotation marks—even 'cards'. Certainly Lawrence was going profoundly below that level of merely social over-individuation. But his apparent assumption that no great writer before him had had this notion is breathtakingly self-centred. What he is pointing to as 'carbon' is either what the French seventeenth century called the 'moi', the self, or what Schopenhauer called the will. In the respect that this element is below social personality, is anonymous and tends to be anti-social, it is related to Freud's 'id'.

But what Shakespeare shows, what Racine shows, is that this force of basic human nature, this will or self, is universal and anonymous only in the abstract. You may find carbon in a pure state, or you may produce it by a chemical process. You can't produce the self or the will in a pure state except by generalizing. In life we only have my self and my will or your self and your will. What is strange is that these are inseparable from me and you, and not reproducible. We all have selves and wills in exactly the same way as we all have faces, voices, and fingerprints : unique.

This is the fundamental philosophical or ethical importance of the notion of 'character'. It *is* individuality. Any great artist has to cope with it. He cannot do so with Lawrence's chemical analogy, useful as it is. It was indeed Lawrence who showed why not, when he talked about his immediately related notion of 'life'. This is not, he says, a force like electricity, which can be generated, or transformed, or stored. It is only found in the individual living human being, and the life of that being *is* that being. One can retort upon Lawrence that the 'life' of a character is certainly not the stable ego : it is the whole person living in time, and possibly being unstable : people do change, and not only by maturing. The 'carbon' of which he speaks is a theoretical construct, related to 'human nature'. This serves generalizing purposes, and shrewd generalizations have been made by moralists. But as soon as we are talking about individuation we are out of the realm of moral generalities and into the realm of dramatists and novelists.

A sense of the limitations of any art form, its conventions, is essential. Perhaps there was a real confusion, in Bradley's mind, about the degree of 'reality' of a work of art, especially a play. We have to remember that these are only words spoken by people moving about on a stage and that we are building up a network of inference from them. They seem to evoke, among other things, a sense of the moral and psychic reality of the people who speak them. This is the basic dramatic convention. But if the characters are speaking poetry of Shakespearean richness and immediacy, the sense that we are in direct contact with the movement of another mind, or will, is very powerful. Yet it is equally the case that Shakespeare is not simply wanting to give us a sense of what it is to be Macbeth or Othello. He has set them in a dramatic whole which produces related characters, contrasts, opposites : the overall intention is to 'situate' or 'place' the protagonist so that we are not simply taken over by him. The large intention of the play is to convey some specific complex experience which reflects and modifies a sense of life as a whole.

To go back to my analyses of Macbeth, I have claimed that the poetry represents, as only such poetry can, the movement of a consciousness, and it is recognizably 'Macbeth's', not Shakespeare's, not ours. The effect of the entire play is to give us that sustained contact with his self-disclosure, in words. This is, surely, 'character in action' in the deep sense of the word. It has nothing to do with being over-individuated, still less with being grotesque; but it does mean being this imagined individual who is 'real' to us in some way related to our sense of real people.

I think it is a common experience of *Macbeth*, read by young people, that they are intoxicated by this sense of 'being' Macbeth. He is one of the parts we all think we can act, because the words given him, and therefore given us, so 'explain' him that to read them and to feel them is to 'be' him. (I have used quotation marks in these sentences to suggest conventional senses of the words used.) It is a much slower process to detach oneself : to come to feel that it is a terrible thing to be Macbeth—to be locked within those limitations, to have done those things, and to have wasted that power. Hence, I think, the extraordinary domination of the play : it does, as few plays do, hold in balance the essential capacity of the dramatist to enter into an imagined being and to take us with him, and his capacity *also* to set that central consciousness in a constellation which prevents our sympathy becoming a collective madness of total identification. It is a salutary schizophrenia which allows us to hear the words as they are spoken (as we speak them) : to hear the element of rant, of violence, of cruelty, of ultimate smallness, blindness. This is our judgement of Macbeth, which springs from and counterbalances our insight into him. It is a moral faculty, and is based on our capacity to do similar things in the real world. It could not be otherwise. If our sympathies were entirely dominated by the dramatist's capacities to orchestrate his score, we should be entirely in his power : we should have no standpoint from which to judge it; we should be open to diametrically opposite promptings from others with appropriate gifts; we should just be weathercocks.

An interest in 'character' then, is an interest in drama. Others might qualify that by saying 'one kind of drama', but I would reply 'The highest kind of drama, and specifically Shakespearean tragedy'. The important instances of 'the dramatic' in Shakespeare cannot, I think, be divorced—or at any rate in Shakespeare's tragedies *are* not divorced—from their origin in an imagined complex and evolving centre of consciousness. This is not a playing-card allegorical viewpoint, nor a sketchily outlined human type, not a grotesque—because we could not identify ourselves to the necessary degree with any of those. Tragedy does demand the tension between identification and judgment at a level which really shakes the established ego.

It is easy therefore largely to agree with hints F. R. Leavis throws out in his classic essay 'Tragedy and the "Medium" ', in particular the remarks about tragedy as not confirming people in their own sense of an approved and final social self in which they are separate from others. But I want also to qualify the agreement. Barriers are not broken down in that disturbing but fruitful way if you are not offered anything complex enough. You are not shaken, though you may be mildly admonished, by an allegory. Indeed, if you happen to approve of the allegorical message you may be dangerously confirmed in your separateness. Only another consciousness of equal complexity can offer a challenge to your own: to enter into one and then be annihilated in it, as you are in *Macbeth*, is the only challenge that drama can offer which is near the same level of seriousness as the challenges that life inflicts.

It is certainly true that the equivalent force of the whole dramatic world in which Macbeth lives and dies is an essential element of the process. The valuable element of modern criticism, which insists on the totality of the experience, the interrelatedness, the symphonic structure, will not now be jettisoned in any shift of critical position. We need, rather, to combine the critical insights available to us, both traditional and modern. There is no need to fall into the either/or trap. It is, I believe, the case that an interest in theme can, indeed must, be related to the interest in 'character'.

Otherwise we fall into comforting assurances of the kind that it seems to me even Leavis approaches—though I don't say that he falls into the trap. He writes:

74

> By [Macbeth's] plunge into crime, taken in fatal ignorance of his
> nature . . . he confounded 'this little state of man', and the im-
> personal order from which it is inseparable. It is not on his
> extinction after a tale of sound and fury, signifying nothing, that
> the play ends, and his valedictory nihilism is the vindication of
> the moral and spiritual order he has outraged, and which is re-
> established in the close.

That's all right then, we might be tempted to say to ourselves, as
Macduff comes in at the end with Macbeth's head; the moral and
spiritual order is vindicated and re-established. It seems to me too
close to the appeal to convention again : we have been made aware
that the Elizabethans were very keen to vindicate such orders. So
our scholarship and our complacency are both more firmly established.

It links with instructions that we ought to leave the theatre feeling
that our 'vitality' has been 'enhanced'—words that Leavis is prepared to accept, and again words which might be taken as invitations
to the reinforcement of the ego. It might be much more appropriate
to go out feeling deeply shocked (as at the end of *Lear*); but if the
feeling is often more positive than that, it still seems to me that one
ought to feel subdued at the end of *Macbeth*.

The key is the degree to which we feel ourselves akin to him. If he
is only a criminal, we have merely seen a five-act come-uppance.
The 'poetry', however, is in one aspect what takes us inside him,
so that it is extremely difficult to distance ourselves, so that we are
strongly tempted to feel as he feels, so that the ultimate need to distance ourselves is a shock, and we are left with a balance of feelings
which is not far from self-division.

If at the end of the play Macbeth were merely offering a variant
of the dying speeches I anthologized earlier—offering the standard
Elizabethan Senecan self-stiffenings, the rhetoric of the self on the
anvil willing itself to be harder than the hammer, and if Shakespeare
were endorsing that, then the last speech would be a 'philosophical'
utterance of a low order. It is not; yet an odd reservation remains
in Leavis's reply. In his alienation from the ranting criminal Macbeth, what is different from his alienation from Othello? Of that
play he says in the other great essay, 'Diabolic Intellect and the Noble
Hero',

even *Othello* . . . is poetic, a dramatic poem, and not a psychological novel written in dramatic form and draped in poetry, *but* [my italics] relevant discussion of its tragic significance will nevertheless be mainly a matter of character-analysis.

I think that is true, yet I don't see that this separates *Othello* from *Macbeth* or *Hamlet* or *Lear* or *Antony and Cleopatra*. So why the 'but'? It seems as if the notion 'poetic drama' is here both consistent and inconsistent with an interest in character-analysis. I go back to a key sentence in the first essay :

> The control over Shakespeare's words in *Macbeth* . . . is a complex dramatic theme vividly and profoundly realized—not thought of, but possessed imaginatively in its concreteness so that, as it grows in specificity, it in turn possesses the poet's mind and commands expression.

Yes; and indeed the 'complex theme' would subsume the characterization, which is part of the whole. But if the characterization is not itself sufficiently complex, the play does just become a matter of the cosmic order re-establishing itself—and let me be blunt and say that that can be a boring and abstract process, a reification not essentially different from the comforting Hegelian dialectic that Bradley found in Shakespearean drama, or neo-classical poetic justice, or the old *hamartia-hubris-nemesis* process that we learn about in primers on Greek tragedy : all of them invitations to feel we understand and to be confirmed in that security.

So it is very difficult to talk about tragedy, and Leavis with characteristic tact made his essay a series of hints, tangential insights, heads of discussion. It remains true, I think, that without some firm sense of character you automatically tend to overstress in tragedy the schematic notion of a cosmic order re-establishing itself, which can be a drily cheering thought; or you fall into the Nietzschean trap of being vitally enhanced by assenting to the death of someone you are prepared to write off, and don't identify yourself with. The two temptations are related; what is common to them is thinking that mere individuals are not important. It is a trick of self-saving alienation; it saves you from feeling pain. Modern criticism and modern scholarship have invited us to assent to corresponding formal or historic preoccupations : the organic form which conveys a theme through stylized characters; the image-chain which symbolizes that

76

theme and is sustained by all the characters; the intellectual pre-occupation of the age; the automatic response of the contemporary audience. These too can cauterize tragedy by short-circuiting a full response to the poetry. My analysis of passages from *Macbeth* was intended to lead back to such a response : to make the play something you feel as it goes on, not something which you vigilantly forestall with your acquired 'approach'. The insight needs to be supported by an account of *Othello* which shows how the admitted element of 'character' in that play goes quite naturally with the admitted notion of 'poetic drama'—how *Othello* and *Macbeth* are related.

5

Othello

There are important disagreements about how *Othello* the play is to be understood. The basic question is : are we to see Othello the man as a noble and fundamentally sympathetic but simple and trusting nature, fatally misled by the diabolic malevolence of Iago; or are we to see him as a man whose murderous jealousy springs from an internal source, a failure of his own nature, so that Iago has only to touch certain psychic triggers for this weakness to display itself? Some scholars might rephrase this : they would say that Othello is portrayed within the convention of the heroic soldier figure, bluff and a little simple; and he is misled by a conventionally Machiavellian figure who rejoices in destruction.

The interest of the discussion is precisely this : that the play forces upon us the issue of its own interpretation. There is no preface by Shakespeare telling us what to think, and no character in the play whose function is to be a *raisonneur*, a commonsense person who represents a rational view which may be the author's. The persons who most persistently press interpretations upon us are Othello and Iago. The fact that between them they encompass a disaster leading to more than one death suggests that they do have a good deal to explain, but that as interested parties, indeed responsible ones (in the sense that they would be responsible in a court of law) we must listen to their self-extenuations with a degree of judiciousness. We are in fact challenged to reach a verdict.

It is therefore easy to contend that this play is valuably like life. There too we see people acting disastrously, and giving an account of themselves which ranges from 'I was quite right to do it' to 'I am not responsible for my actions', through 'I was fatally misled by a wicked manipulator'. We have to make judgements which necessarily involve deciding why the person, being what he is, did what he did. A drama which does justice to that situation represents a very high

reach of art : indeed I would argue that the drama which forces
on the audience the problem of judging, yet makes it as difficult as
it is in life, can be of a higher order than an art—like the novel—
where the author has it in his power to tell the reader what to think.
So the argument about the meaning of *Othello* is a tribute to its
force. I contend, nonetheless, that an interpretation is asked of us,
and that (as in life) the cause of justice demands a verdict. So we
are not allowed to say that to understand all is to forgive all. To
understand correctly is, in appropriate cases, to condemn, or there
can be no morality. To find other people disagreeing is to be forced
to reconsider, and then possibly to ground the condemnation more
convincingly.

One interest of *Othello*, then, is that it presents us with this entirely
mature form of drama, where characters have to be judged by the
criteria of . . . well, what? All we have of Othello, Shaw pointed out,
is what he says. He went on to say therefore 'he does not exist'. Not
so; for one thing we do have other evidence : since we also have
what the other people say, and, most convincingly, we have what
Othello *does*. And what do we 'have' of anybody in real life? What
they say; what others say of them; what they do; our built-up sense
of them which reaches us from such sources and is incorporated into
our judgement of them. A well-portrayed and well-acted character
in a drama is valuably representative of a real person in precisely
that sense.

And although we have our stereotypes, including stereotypes of
military men, we know very well that the generic picture can be
false and misleading. We expect nobody to be merely true to type.
The conventional soldier-figure is not found in a pure state in life,
and would not be in the least interesting in the drama. It has been
argued by scholars that if we are not to take Othello at his self-
valuation or as a conventional figure, then he becomes much more
difficult to act. So he does, and a good thing too. But how does the
actor portray lack of self knowledge, 'inauthenticity' (to use the vogue
word), actual self-deception? It can't be done, they say, it is strictly
unactable : thus writing off the important plays of Racine, Molière,
Chekhov and, of course, Shakespeare. And indeed it was Olivier's
very willed performance of Othello, constructed (one supposes) after
reading Leavis or Eliot, and full of signs to the audience that something peculiar was going on, which suggested that actors at any rate

79

had better not be so conscious of what's motivating the character that they feel obliged to act him with one foot outside the part. If Othello is, as I think, a self-deceiving man, then it is important to play him with a desperate sincerity—out of which one might, for instance, murder an innocent person.

Suppose that Othello demonstrates some fundamental workings of the self : especially the kind of insecurity which fluctuates between dominance and dependence in its relationships, needs that kind of relation to be supported sexually, and is in danger of flying into the extreme of wild jealousy if threatened in that precarious stability, or thinking it is. Iago then becomes a person who gets a satisfaction from manipulating that process, partly because it gives him a sense of power, partly because it proves him right about something. Right about what? Not just about Othello's reactions. Iago comes across from the beginning as a gross, an extreme, cynic about human actions and emotions; it is borne in on us as he proceeds that he *needs* to prove something about the falseness or weakness of other people's attachments. This is not just because he is a bold bad man or a machiavel in the old convention. He has grown out of that convention, certainly, but in mentioning Richard III's opening soliloquy I touched on ways in which the convention was acquiring greater human reality. Richard, arbitrarily punished by the world by being born an ugly physical nature, responds by becoming an ugly soul, and pays the world back in spite. Iago takes that exploration of the self further. He does indeed say of Cassio at one point :

> He hath a daily beauty in his life
> That makes me ugly.

This is a give-away—indeed it might be said that here Shakespeare nudges us rather hard : it is doubtful if an Iago could really see the beauty and his own ugliness, for that convicts him of being what he is. It is his main activity to deny this, and to do so by denying the beauty as well. Hence his cynicism. Cassio, for intance, is 'almost damned in a fair wife'. What does that mean? As we ponder it, we see that he is implying that beauty leads naturally to unchastity : Cassio will therefore automatically be deceived, like everyone ele. This may need to be proved, if the world seems likely to prove one wrong.

The real dangerousness of Iago's nature is that anything that proves him ugly, proves him wrong, proves beautiful and true, must be destroyed, because he cannot have it go on living and proving him wrong. This, we see after a time, is an operation of *jealousy* : and though their jealousy is of different kinds, Othello and Iago are linked by it. More : what we call by one word 'jealousy', and think of as one thing, is much more various. If I can't have it, then you shan't have it; I shall break it. That is the child's jealousy. The adult's jealousy, in Othello, is 'Be what I want you to be in relation to me, or I shall be violent to you.' In Iago it is 'be like me, or you prove me vile'. Be contemptible or you wrove me wrong. If I fear you will prove me vile, wrong and therefore ultimately lonely, I shall destroy you, or your attachments to others. This undercurrent of feeling : be like me, be what I want you to be, is the private and personal equivalent of communal emotion—tribalism. Shakespeare leads us to that in his language : Iago's deepest utterance is

> Poor and content is rich, and rich enough;
> But riches fineless is as poor as winter
> To him that ever fears he shall be poor.
> Good heaven the souls of all my *tribe* defend
> From jealousy.

At the end of the play Othello knows he is a member too—

> one whose hand
> Like the base Indian threw a pearl away
> Richer than all his *tribe*.

The word 'rich' is used by both, and the word 'tribe'. These are elements in a language which they share, and I must now analyse some of it, getting away from this rather schematic psychology. It indicates another general point : Iago and Othello are audibly related by their language at a very deep level—the level, I would say, at which we are all related. If you have ever thought another person ought to share your tastes and interests or your fortune, have pressed that person to do so, been conscious of being undermined in a tiny way when they refused or upset when their path diverged from yours —even in a trivial matter—then you are a distant relative of Iago's. If you have ever felt emotional or sexual jealousy, you are more closely related to Othello. These are operations of the basic self— what Lawrence was talking of as the 'carbon' of the universal human ego that underlies personality. Three hundred years before Lawrence,

Shakespeare was showing greater knowledge in these matters, and using a language which made it possible to do in the drama what Lawrence thought could only be done in the novel.

What is Iago saying in that curious speech where 'poor' and 'rich' arise as natural inversions of each other? The words recur like an ostinato. He is saying that to be, like himself, conscious of being 'poor' but happy in the state, is to be secure in the sense that those who are at rock bottom have nothing to fear. The rich (those who love and are loved) have to fear being beggared or robbed. Be therefore like me, Iago, loveless and unloved; therefore self-insured against emotional loss. It is an appeal to a sense of insecurity, and Othello is insecure. But he is also rich : he is loved. Iago wants, needs, to bring him down to rock bottom, where they will both be members of the tribe. This tribe need feel no jealousy, he implies—not allowing for the fact that tribesmen (like himself) are insecure, jealous, in the presence of people not in the tribe. These must be made to belong, or destroyed.

But he is talking the language of the will, that is to say a metaphorical language. We have here an opposition between poverty and wealth (the two terms convert into each other by natural mental operations). 'Poor as winter' is a striking folk-phrase, which naturally associates poverty with coldness and sterility; overtly saying something about being 'deprived', it may covertly say something about spiritual coldness at heart.

Othello's last-but-one speech brings back the notion of wealth in the specific image of the 'pearl richer than all his tribe'. Here the thing of value is made specific, a jewel. Pearls come, mysteriously, from the sea. Almost at the very beginning of the play, Othello, just married, had said to Iago

> For know, Iago,
> But that I love the gentle Desdemona
> I would not my unhoused free condition
> Put into circumscription and confine
> For the sea's worth.

The 'sea's worth' is all the treasure it contains and may cast up on shore—or which 'base Indians' may cast back into it. Desdemona *is* the sea's worth, but he does not realize that until too late. Othello's odd remark, as of the bachelor saying goodbye to his freedom, has powerful undertones. If he is 'unhoused' he is unsheltered—from the winter for instance. But he associates being 'housed' with circumscription and confinement—as in a prison, a dungeon. So he rather fears his commitment.

It is a small point, but the play swarms with these little figurative snatches which light up and light each other up and become a tissue of psychic correspondences. The image of wealth, associated with the jewel or pearl Desdemona, naturally enough occurs to her father Brabantio who is a 'possessive' father, jealous, resents her 'loss', and thinks he is 'robbed' by Othello, to whom he says :

> O thou foul thief, where hast thou stowed my daughter?

One stows things in, for instance, barns or garners as well as in holes and corners. Brabantio says of his passionate resentment that

> my particular grief
> Is of so floodgate and o'erbearing nature
> That it engluts and swallows other sorrows . . .

It is therefore like a sea, a flood forced through a narrow channel; and this image will recur too. Convinced at last that Othello genuinely has Desdemona's heart, but not reconciled to it, Brabantio says gruffly

> Come hither, Moor :
> I here do give thee that with all my heart
> Which but thou hast already, with all my heart
> I would keep from thee. (*To Desdemona*) For your sake, jewel,
> I am glad at soul I have no other child,
> For thy escape would teach me tyranny . . .

Having, and giving, and keeping for oneself, and keeping from others; being a rich man; being a miser; being a beggar; being a thief—these are fundamental comparisons in a play which asks : what does it mean to love and be loved, therefore in some sense to have, to possess, another person, or to 'win' their love, or to lose it, or to steal it from others? Fundamental also is the notion of value, worth. Desdemona is a pearl, a jewel : her love is beyond price. *Can* it actually be stolen, or *can* it be withheld, as by a miser, from others? Does she not bestow it freely; and may she not therefore withdraw it? Is she to be valued because she is 'owned', or simply for what she is? Does Othello truly value her, if he can be persuaded on mere suspicion to kill her? Does not Iago destroy what he cannot himself have, because deep down he knows he is not *worth* the love of another human being, but cannot bear that knowledge? Does not Othello also come to fear that he is not loved, so that he has really no firm sense of his own worth? Does he not, before our eyes, 'devalue' himself?

I think these remarks are shrewd enough in their way, and worth making in those terms. What I want to try to show, however, is how the language of the play is superior to these limited interpretations of it, and how in Othello's most anguished utterances he is, without self-consciousness (indeed with that kind of consciousness and the consequent restraint utterly in abeyance) pouring out a direct flow from the deepest part of the self. It is the triumph of Shakespeare's art that this supreme display of character portrayal is not merely the documentation of a 'case'. Othello is a representative man, related to the spectator, and audibly linked by his language to the other characters in the play, even Iago.

The storm out of which first Desdemona and then Othello sail into Cyprus is an orchestral prelude to the catastrophe. The 'enchaféd flood' which nearly wrecks them is emblematic of internal storms and floods which are as Brabantio said, of 'floodgate and o'erbearing nature'. The sounds of 'floodgate' are carried on in his next line in 'engluts and swallows' : these are physiological sounds and sensations. Similar sounds echo in Cassio's more formal and somewhat self-admiring oratory :

> Tempests themselves, high seas, and howling winds,
> The guttered rocks and congregated sands,
> Traitors insteeped to clog the guiltless keel
> As having sense of beauty, do omit
> Their mortal natures, letting go safely by
> The divine Desdemona.

'Guttered' and 'congregated' and 'clog the guiltless keel' twist the tongue and catch the ear. A 'guttered' rock has rough channels down which the water of the spent wave runs back foaming to the main sea. But gutters are also associated with filth and poverty (beggars stand in them). 'Congregated' sands are all gluey; things stick in them (keels clog). But congregations are people, and in the next line are 'traitors' lurking for the 'guiltless'. So the suggestion is that there are starving thieves and murderers waiting to rob the jewel Desdemona. Cassio enforces the point a few lines later as she appears:

> O behold,
> The riches of the ship is come on shore!

Who are the thieves and beggars? It is eventually clear that they are Iago, who protests his honest 'poverty', and Othello. The one robs the other by persuading him to throw his jewel away.

The sea churning through the floodgates, the gutters: the notion of a violent tide going through a too narrow channel is a very apt figure for some kinds of passion. The sea is a vast inhuman element out there beyond us, in which we would be swallowed up, engulfed ('englutted' in Brabantio's active phrase). If we have something of the sea in us it is as a suffusing flood which surges up in us. For instance

> *Othello:* O, blood, blood, blood!
> *Iago:* Patience I say; your mind perhaps may change.
> *Othello:* Never, Iago; like to the Pontic sea
>   Whose icy current and compulsive course
>   Ne'er feels retiring ebb, but keeps due on
>   To the Propontic and the Hellespont;
>   Even so my bloody thoughts with violent pace
>   Shall ne'er look back, ne'er ebb to humble love
>   Till that a capable and wide revenge
>   Swallow them up.

The basic comparison is with the tide which surges between the Mediterranean and Black Sea, through the narrows of the Dardanelles, the sea of Marmara, the Bosporus. This mere geography is internalized. The 'pont . . . pont . . . pont' is like something being banged against the sides of what it passes through. The 'icy current' is a winter-chilled bloodstream obsessively fixed on a violent course of action; it will not turn back from its intention ('ne'er feels retiring ebb'). But shed blood also flows only one way. The effect of 'capable and wide' is extraordinary; the achievement of revenge is a release, like passing from the internal narrows out, liberated, into some enormous psychic sea, which 'engluts and swallows'—and there, with huge satisfaction, he sees the bodies turn under the surface and sink. It is a glimpse of homicidal madness.

The channel to and from the eternal sea of unhuman uncon-sciousness can shift into other strange mutations, by association with other image-complexes. For instance, Iago starts a theme when he says

> Utter my thoughts! Why, say they are vile and false—
> As where's that palace whereinto foul things
> Sometimes intrude not? Who has a breast so pure
> But some uncleanly apprehensions
> Keep leets and law-days, and in session sit
> With meditations lawful?

The foul things in the palace, contrasted with what is pure and clean (like fresh water, for instance) are creatures of the sewers. There is a nexus here of images of filth, of foul smells, and farmyard copulations. Iago and Othello exchange these in a fearful duet where they develop each other's obsessions:

> Exchange me for a goat
> When I shall turn the business of my soul
> To such exsufflicate and blown surmise . . .

> Foh! One may smell, in such, a will most rank,
> Foul disproportion, thoughts unnatural.

The themes come together first in one of Othello's most revolting utterances:

> O curse of marriage
> That we can call these delicate creatures ours,
> And not their appetites. I had rather be a toad,
> And live upon the vapour of a dungeon,
> Than keep a corner in the thing I love
> For others' uses.

We have to face what he is saying. He would become a foul thing in his own palace, rather than . . . what? Share her sexually : this envisaged specifically as seeing others excrete upon her, he standing by as a toad, watching, and living upon the vapour. Jealousy there-fore turns the palace into a dungeon, turns lovemaking to copro-philia. People in dungeons have to do things in the corner, have to because there is no choice. Toads living upon this vapour are vile beyond words; but he sees himself as one. By an extraordinarily rich and horrible imaginative stroke on Shakespeare's part Othello's obsessive and fascinated disgust is conveyed to us. She has become a 'thing', and the 'others' are plural.

Towards the end of the play he tries to convey his terrible and disgusting misery to Desdemona, and it comes out in a choked flow where the themes coalesce. She asks why he is weeping: is she the cause?

> *Othello:* Had it pleased heaven
> To try me with affliction; had they rained
> All kinds of sores and shames on my bare head,
> Steeped me in poverty to the very lips,
> Given to captivity me and my utmost hopes,
> I should have found in some place of my soul
> A drop of patience; but alas! to make me
> A fixéd figure for the time of scorn
> To point his slow unmoving finger at!
> Yet I could bear that too : well, very well.
> But there, where I have garnered up my heart,
> Where either I must live or bear no life,
> The fountain from the which my current runs,
> Or else dries up—to be discarded thence!
> Or keep it as a cistern for foul toads
> To knot and gender in!

By a self-dramatizing trick he sees himself first as a Lear or Job, out in the open, without shelter, being rained on (poor as winter). But the water turns at once to sewage or infection, becomes 'sores and shames'. By another instant transformation it is a rising tide in which he is 'steeped' (that word again, first met in Cassio's 'traitors insteeped'). 'To the very lips' with its mimetic movements suggests that he hardly dare speak, or the tide of filth will come into his mouth. He is indeed housed, unfree, in that dungeon again (given to captivity) chained underground in the castle's sewer. Then an extraordinary modification in the imagery occurs : all this, he claims, is outside him, not *his* current, *his* tide. Indeed he is heroically locked around, he can find it somewhere, a drop of a pure essence, 'patience' envisaged as clear water, preserved from the filth. That image dissolves, and he is once more chained immobile, but now exposed as a kind of shameful statue-sundial where the sun never moves. He conquers that resentment, and moves into a summating figure where his notion of grace and purity and his notion of filth and betrayal conflict : both thought of as liquid elements.

'But there, where I have garnered up my heart' is at first positive : garners are for harvested corn, the riches of summer. The notion however carries a subthought of miserliness, of hoarding to himself his riches, in contrast to the 'poverty' in which he is steeped to the lips.

> Where either I must live or bear no life
> The fountain from which my current flows
> Or else dries up—to be discarded thence !

A stone garner could be like an underground cistern, meant for pure water, fed by a source. So indeed his dungeon-self was meant to be flushed by the current of his love for her, or to receive that pure water, the drop of patience. The image here is agonizingly felt : this is his need for her—dependent or possessive, but nonetheless a true need. He envisages her love as cleansing, refreshing, the water of life. A fountain is kindly and sustaining : in clear contrast either to the sewer, the dungeon, or the tidal wave hurtling through the narrows. But his nature and his obsession are such that this master-image is instantly and hideously transformed back into the cistern in which the foul toads knot and gender. We are back with repulsion, stink, vileness, copulation : and all produced from within. Desdemona has done nothing to justify this flow of filth, which springs entirely from Othello's lack of faith in her, therefore inability to value her or believe that she values him.

In so far as Iago is responsible—and to a great degree he is—for provoking this collapse of a once apparently noble stature, he is envisaged at the end of the play as an inhuman force. Lodovico addresses him :

> O Spartan dog,
> More fell than anguish, hunger, or the sea ! . . .

The words seem spontaneous, but come from depths of understanding. The Spartans practised a kind of willed poverty; but this person is an animal who brings down those he seems to follow at heel. Anguish and hunger are the proper portion of the poor (who are not 'poor and content', but envious and dangerous) : the sea is the universal swallower-up of all identity, and impersonal as winter.

The figures pass into each other by entirely natural transitions as if an internal kaleidoscope turned and the constituents of the psyche, themselves unchanging, take up the new patterns of the moment's stress. It is, I believe, useful and valuable to follow the kind of analysis I have presented here if it gives the reader or spectator an enhanced sense of what is going on, and makes the significance clearer. The danger is that the analysis may be accepted as substitute or entire meaning. I have partly pressed out into the open, in certain words, what goes on in the mind as a simultaneity of contending feelings, as flux or wild expansion, or repulsion. These things can be felt as a riot of images, and they are here conventionally conveyed as a succession of rhythmic metaphors : essentially 'mixed' metaphors, because the feelings themselves are mixed. Shakespeare's verse, the convention, allows an extraordinarily faithful metaphorical rendering if one also accepts the convention that characters can verbalize these mental events as they take place—that they actually have the verbal power to do it adequately. (This convention leads to the common and not foolish fallacy that leading characters are 'poets'. They are not, any more than Mozart's or Verdi's or Wagner's are both composers and singers.)

The point of the convention is the access it gives to the mind— or rather something deeper than the mind considered as mere intelligence or concept-wielding device. The consciousness revealed here is like a screen, or more exactly a stage, on which internal forces are performing a synaesthetic or operatic sequence : not just a visual show, but a tonal and rhythmic one as well.

And though the thematic structure—the exchange, development, inversion, combination, metamorphosis of images—is profoundly impressive, very beautiful and leads one to contemplate the whole play as a 'structure', an organic entity which is deeply considered and exquisitely through-composed, this is not something merely formal. It is fairly easy to elaborate a symbolic form : to have themes and repeat them and play variations on them. It can be very boring when it is merely deliberate : and nothing is more boring than the criticism which goes through a work, hermeneutic Jack Horner, hooking out the themes one by one. Nor is it much better to point out that the themes 'mean' this or that : it merely turns the plum-pudding into an algebraical plum-pudding, where this always equals *that*. Then why not say *that*, and say it plainly? is the inevitable response. We don't want plums in suet, nor algebra. The themes must therefore have immediacy : correspond to our sense of what actually goes on inside. They have to work as themselves, not as their 'meanings'. They have to have that Shakespearean volatility in which they pass into each other with a speed greater than that of mere thought. They have to have a kind of indeterminacy in which it is clear that they are more active, more significant than their prose paraphrase— the indeterminacy being a richness or valency directly related to that immediacy, volatility, ductility. Finally they have to be speakable : they have to come out as a credible self-revelation by a convincing character of adequate depth who is credited dramatically with this power to verbalize, and is also highly individuated.

That the words are 'speakable' raises the question : are they 'hearable'? I mean, can we hear in them, as they are spoken, all that I have been extracting from them? It is a real point. My analysis is leisurely, the result of brooding over the words. There is a no-nonsense approach which says that that sort of thing is all very well in the armchair or in the study, where one pores over the printed text. But in the theatre the words are spoken aloud in succession : they make their instantaneous effect, which fades as fast as it is received. Can we possibly take in a charge of meaning as complex as the one unpacked, layer by layer, in a detailed analysis? There is a temptation to say no; the theatre deals in the immediate.

It is a serious argument, and deserves a reply. The first element of the reply must be equally blunt : do the words mean what the analyst says they mean, or don't they? If they don't mean what he says, what *do* they mean? I can only ask, are my analyses convincing? The reply might be : well, the words mean something rather like that, but also rather less, since we can't take in so much all at once. The answer is : you don't have to, all at once. If the drama were entirely ephemeral, and meant to be seen only once, it could not convey so much, except to people who have such retentive memories that they can take large tracts of the play home with them and brood on them. (Not so unlikely an event, for those who re-collect how in ordinary life they may at times have brooded on what another person meant when he or she said *that*.) Plays are printed not only to provide prompt books : they are meant to be read and thought about. They are above all meant to be seen again and again—and this would not happen if it were not a universal experience that the more you see it the more you see in it : to the point where you have, in one sense of the word, a classic theatre. As A. W. Schlegel said of the French classical drama :

> in external dignity, quickness, correctness of memory, and in a wonderful degree of propriety and elegance in the delivery of verse, the best French actors are hardly to be surpassed ... The extremely fastidious taste of a Paris pit and the wholesome severity of the journalists, excite in them a spirit of incessant emulation; and the circumstance of acting a number of classical works which for generations have been in the possession of the stage, contributes also greatly to their excellence ... As the spectators have these words nearly by heart, their whole attention may be directed to the acting ...

What that means is that the audience, knowing the work, come to know also more of what it contains; and that implies that judging the acting means judging how much and how well the content is being conveyed—how much the actor seems to know of what it means or how much he can instinctively convey it. The analogy again is with music. The actor rehearsing a play is like a performer learning his piece of music : he does not learn 'how to play' something which he already 'understands'. He learns to understand it, so that he may then play it well. The audience then learns to hear it. A good performer can spend a lifetime learning his repertory : what he is displaying is not 'technique' but inwardness with the work. Listening to the great performer is learning more about the work, understanding it better. So with a good actor. We do not question, I think, the music critic who attempts to show ever deeper subtleties of structure in great music; or we do not argue against the attempt by saying 'we can't hear all that in a single performance'. That is to underestimate the ultimate power of the performing arts, which inheres in the paradox that we listen to this one ephemeral performance now and consider it as an attempt to provide the ideal performance which is never realizable. To argue otherwise about the greatest drama ever written is to devalue it. Shakespeare is our great classic author, and we ought to try to possess him in as much of his inexhaustible depth as we can manage. My final point must therefore logically be that I have *understated* the depth and complexity, have made simple and crude what cannot ultimately be paraphrased.

A related point, which needs to be faced, is that music and poetry, by their nature, can only be talked about in words, or in other words.

91

This inevitably leads to discrepancies in the descriptions; and so to occasions where one person says 'it means A' where another person says 'it means B.' This is to be expected, but it does not imply that the medium has no meaning, so that one throws up one's hands and says 'Oh, all right. Anything you say'. The difference of opinion has to be argued out, and by reference to the governing features of the context.

So, for instance, when John Dover Wilson says of '. . . Vaulting ambition, which o'erleaps itself / And falls on the other . . .' that it shows Macbeth imagining himself vaulting into the saddle, overdoing it, and landing on the other side of the horse, I would say that he has not got it right. In the previous lines 'I have no spur / To prick the sides of my intent, but only . . .' Macbeth is imagining himself already *in* the saddle, and urging his horse to the jump. There is no certainty here; the two readings are possible; but I would argue for mine as the fuller realization of the whole passage. Readers will judge; and if enough of them agree with me, that becomes an accepted sense of the passage. It is the nature of the metaphorical tissue of Shakespeare's writing that we are led inwards, and made to feel our way along the network. It cannot be an arbitrary process, nor is it the indulgence of a fantasy-spinning armchair-reader elaborating pseudo-significances. It is the effort to feel ourselves into the imagined mind of Macbeth, as he speaks these words.

My term 'speakable' returns us to Shakespeare's gift, which is to get so much into words, which do to a remarkable degree assist the performer. In fact they are very often what used simply to be called 'beautiful' : the great moments in Shakespeare are usually affecting and striking in an immediate way, but the surface leads us inwards. This power, in the play *Othello,* is an almost dreadful gift. Othello is revealed as an extraordinary individuality. He is very nearly a 'case'. What ties him to humanity is also, strangely, what ties him to Iago : what ties both of them to us—a relationship we are not eager to acknowledge. We want to turn away from both of them : the horrible victory of one and the horrible defeat of the other. The language they share reveals depths in them which underlie their individuality : underlie ours too.

6

French Classical Tragedy: Racine's *Phedre*

There is a general assumption—has been since the eighteenth century —that French classical tragedy is a uniform product turned out by a two-headed writer, Corneille and Racine. It was a drama (so this account goes) which stuck very closely to neo-classical models of decorum, and was couched in a very regular form of verse: Alexandrines, hexameters in couplets. It is monotonous and grand, but has moments of rather striking elevation, and moments of pathos. But it does not speak much to us today, largely because the verse is cold and formal, and the characters are seen from the outside as heroic social personages.

It is all highly 'classical': set very often in Rome or Greece, and using the Greek pantheon as a source of mythical allusion. It sticks to the unities of time and place. This means that the play opens when some long-impending crisis finally arrives, and a succession of admittedly well-plotted events follows in rapid succession. Ideally the whole action falls within the time taken to play it. Everything also happens in one place: some vague antechamber in a royal palace where people may naturally be waiting for someone else and may fall naturally into conversation. And it *is* all talk: nothing happens, but the people emote to each other in very formal terms. A may then say to B, 'Ah, but I see X approaching' and leave, because X is hateful to him. X does indeed approach, and you are in the next scene. X may then be left by B for some other carefully explained but natural-seeming reason, and X may then soliloquize, saying what he feels about what he has just heard: this is scene iii. When these successive entrances and exits lead to an empty stage, that is the end of the act. The next act takes place on the same set and has the same general strategy.

Nobody gets stabbed on stage, indeed no violent action—no essential physical action of any sort—takes place. If something happens out in the world, this is reported to the characters, who then consider and react to this change of fortune. There may be very long speeches containing such narratives. Otherwise the speech takes two forms: passages of verbal fencing, in which people are testing each other in some way, and striving for an advantage; or occasional outbursts in which a central character explains why he or she is torn with emotion. The first form tends to be neat, formal, musical, and quite exciting if you are inferring motivation. The second is like an aria.

The emotions by which these people are torn are essentially internal conflicts. Certain dualities are invoked; the characters seem all to have been studying Descartes' *Traité des passions*, and are aware that they are a body and a soul, a reason and a heart, a rational social will and an opposite inclination. These dual principles regularly threaten to split the person into separate elements: it is his heroic function to dominate an impulse, usually some form of love, and to return to a state of unity which he and his fellow aristocrats can approve. If not, he will die. Or alternatively, and very often, he must accept death or court it as a way of showing how heroically he wants that unity of the self, that victory of the social will over the anarchic personal impulsive will.

We admire, we understand, we may not be much moved, or not by this parody-generalization, anyway. The parody itself was created by neo-classical theorists who used Corneille and Racine in a propagandist argument about the general rules of dramatic art: urged that the two great tragedians had always stuck to the rules, and so should everyone else. But though the rules can in general be deduced from their practice, both these writers were individuals and men of genius. They bent the rules often enough when it suited them (partly because the concrete had not yet set: there was still flexibility). More to the point, the mere sticking to the rules was not the important thing about their drama. One could say of Racine in particular that the conventions of his drama gave him a medium so entirely agreed between him and his audience that he could forget about them; the medium became transparent and he could concentrate on what really concerned him. This was to show through the drama how the human will worked in this central character or that.

English renaissance drama was essentially popular, as we saw.

It could use a vernacular language in which it was said of a king

> The skipping king, he ambled up and down . . .

and that he was

> but as the cuckoo is in June,
> Heard, not regarded.

A queen contemplating a great crime could think of Heaven seeing her by 'peeping' through 'the blanket of the dark'. Now it is not merely unthinkable to a neo-classical critic that kings should behave in an undignified manner, or even be reported as doing so : it was unthinkable that even undignified behaviour should be described in 'vulgar' language : the natural metaphors of the common tongue.

French classical drama is also not popular in the sense that it is far *less* sophisticated in some ways than the English or Spanish drama. A popular audience can be told 'here is a tower, with a character in it, imprisoned'. It then accepts that this is a tower. The character comes into view above, and speaks to others down below. Or a king comes out on the battlements and speaks to his besiegers, again below. Romeo climbs up to Juliet's room, the dying Antony is hoisted into Cleopatra's mausoleum, and so on. All that balletic energy and imagination is denied to the French stage by the 1660s, by a naive literalism which insists that the spectator is not to be exhorted, as the Prologue in *Henry V* exhorts his audience, to make its imagination work. Lully's *Alceste*—an opera—sounds refreshingly familiar to English audiences because people go on shipboard, and move off, and a castle is actually stormed. But you understand that this is already archaic in its time; the opera is taking over spectacular elements which were familiar in stylized form in the ballet or other court entertainments. A rather contemptible mixed-mode is accepted in a mere spectacular entertainment; it would not be possible in the high art of tragedy.

On the other hand, French classical tragedy is like the English drama in that it is conventional and in verse. I have touched on the conventions peculiar to a classicizing theatre, which separate France from England and Spain. The more important common conventions are the use of dramatic verse, and the conventions of aside, soliloquy and tirade. These link the national traditions in respects which are

D

more important than the differences, for they mean that Racine with his quite distinct verse-forms and much more formal and restricted language can nonetheless have some of the same aims as Shakespeare : that the French conventions, like the earlier English ones, evolve in the direction of an *internal* drama, a drama of character, where the self-expression of the major characters is a revelation of the workings of an individual self or will.

In this respect Corneille is genuinely more 'primitive' than Racine. The kind of inwardness with his characters that he reveals is (*mutatis mutandis*) like the inwardness of Shakespeare's predecessors. He is aware that his characters have an interior life; and indeed they talk about it, with strong feeling. The character Rodrigue, the hero of *Le Cid*, who comes forward at the crisis of that play and bursts into a kind of strophic aria, his famous *stances*, beginning

> Percé jusques au fond du cœur . . .

conveys to us that he is torn by the conflict he is undergoing. He has a duty to avenge a slight upon the family honour; he can only do this by killing the father of the woman he loves. This is complex in the sense that the urge to duel is not just a social feeling : it is powerfully bound up with one's personal aggressiveness or sense of pride, including one's self-assurance or self-love. The emotions are therefore not entirely abstract. It remains the case, however, that his mode of self-expression (and that means specifically the verse-forms and the language he is given) cannot make us feel his utterance as directly as we feel Macbeth's, because it is not such that we *can* so feel it. He can't, so to speak, get all of himself directly into his words because they are not metaphorical enough. He remains at a remove : undoubtedly heroic, interesting, noble, vigorous and other things of that sort, but not to any important degree a self or will that we are in direct possession of. We have no temptation to feel (if we speak his words) that we are him because we feel the whole of him speaking them. The actor has the specific task of bringing this role to life : he has to create it by adding something, not by simply realizing in performance what Corneille has written.

A great deal of Corneille's drama is effective, even moving. But the modern taste—and I think it is correct—is for Corneille's gift of sardonic utterance in, for instance, *Nicomède*, where a group of worldly courtiers speak to each other, often in tones of abrasive contempt. This is essentially a social mode, where utterance is a weapon. It gives nothing away about the speaker except his attitude to the person he is speaking to : and even this by strange inversions where the tone tells you not to accept the apparent sense (he may not be expressing a direct meaning, but a sarcastic or ironic one). It denotes a self-contained person who is actually withholding himself, defining himself negatively, and this is a mode of comedy.

Corneille is also primitive if you think, as I do, that the essentially heroic view of human nature in his tragedies is a bit simple. By and large it is true that Corneille's heroes win their battles with themselves. The social self subdues the merely personal impulse : the implied challenge to the audience is 'There ! manage that, and you too are a noble person. Approve it, and you endorse the values of a heroic nobility'.

An aristocratic society confident of its values does indeed need to see them exemplified and sustained in its art-forms. Such is Corneille's role; he gives the French nobility at the high point of French political hegemony a mirror in which it can see itself as vigorous and disciplined; its energy channelled in the direction of its values; self-approval and social approval coinciding. Racine seems to be using the same words and exploring the same conflicts, and producing an entirely different sense.

His drama can be truthfully described by saying that everything in it is used to express the inner workings of his characters; even the most conventional devices. For instance, the device of the *confidant* or *confidante*. This is a person of relatively humble status, attached to the main character as friend or servant or officer. The function of the *confidant* in an inert drama is to ask questions and to be given answers; this is an expository device which enables the dramatist to convey to the audience background information essential to the understanding of the drama. It is highly conventional in that, crudely used, these characters would be telling each other things they already know, or ought to know. In the case of Phèdre, however, her *confidante* Oenone, her former nurse, is a much more active presence. Her role in the action is important : her curiosity, her concern, set the drama in motion. She does not neutrally ask questions : she has an attitude of personal involvement; she probes, indeed nags. Phèdre for her part does not just neutrally answer the questions put to her : one half of her divided self, the clear-sighted half, knows that if she discloses her disastrous passion for her stepson, she is under a social obligation to punish herself for it, and must kill herself. The other part of her, weary of her internal struggle and the loneliness of it, longs to disclose the secret and have it all over with. The reasons are complex : the relief of simply sharing the burden with a sympathetic hearer, the pleasure of being able to pour out her love, if only vicariously, and at bottom the thought that when she has given way and disclosed her guilt, she will then have to purge it, and kill herself anyway. The mere certainty, after the doubtful struggle for self-mastery, will be a relief.

So Oenone in ignorance touches fatal triggers. Phèdre pours out her heart in an enormous painful declaration, which leaves her appeased, in a kind of lucidity, and a reconciliation to her fate. Oenone then has to busy herself to bring Phèdre back to a will to live, and her interventions, always well meant, lead eventually to moral blindness and the false accusation that the stepson Hippolyte has attempted to rape Phèdre.

He too has a *confidant* : his former tutor Théramène, who also busies himself on behalf of his patron; offering advice which is again well-meant but issues from a limited vision. He too prompts a disclosure : it turns out that Hippolyte too is relieved to disburden himself. He too loves where he should not : loves the princess Aricie, a captive descended from a hostile dynasty. His father Thésée, Phèdre's husband, will never approve.

The two first disclosures set a pattern. The great complicating movement of the play follows when Hippolyte is unable to conceal his love for Aricie; he *has* to tell her. It emerges that he is torn because he had a self-image. His father Thésée had been a noted philanderer and adulterer; some complex disgust at the older man's easy and unprincipled sexuality had made Hippolyte vow himself to chastity : he was noted as a kind of ostentatiously virgin prince : Diana's huntsman. Now he finds that he has succumbed to the common law, is seized with longing for Aricie. Finding himself in her presence, and thinking he was only going to take formal leave of her, he cannot stop himself telling her that he is in love with her. Before he knows what he is doing, he is down on his knees, pouring out an avowal, and then brought up short, wondering if he has simply made himself ridiculous.

And while he is in this disarray Phèdre enters and the pattern duplicates itself again. She thinks she is only going to ask him, now that he is king (for Thésée is missing and presumed dead), to be kind to her children, for she fears she has not long to live.

I must now analyse the next 120 lines or so, because only direct contact with the French can give the movement of these two wills or selves at this crucial moment : the greatest scene in French drama.

Act II Scene v

Phèdre's first words, in their simplicity and their honesty, contrast strongly with the courtly disguises Hippolyte and Aricie had been throwing over their self-disclosures. She begins, almost with dread, certainly with a touch of grimness :

> *Phèdre:* Le voici. Vers mon coeur tout mon sang se retire.
> J'oublie, en le voyant, ce que je viens lui dire.
>
> *He is here. All my blood withdraws into my heart.*
> *I forget, seeing him, what I came to say to him.*

> *Oenone:* Souvenez-vous d'un fils qui n'espère qu'en vous.
>
> *Remember that your son depends on you.*

Phèdre collects her forces, and approaches Hippolyte with courteous formality :

> *Phèdre:* On dit qu'un prompt départ vous éloigne de nous,
> Seigneur.
>
> *It is said that you are shortly to leave us, Prince.*

and offers sympathy in their joint loss of Thésée :

> A vos douleurs je viens joindre mes larmes.
>
> *I come to mingle my tears with your grief.*

But she moves immediately away from that tack (he is not weeping; nor is she) and pushes forward her overt or political purpose :

> Je vous viens pour un fils expliquer mes alarmes.
> Non fils n'a plus de père ;
>
> *I come to explain my concern for my son.*
> *My son no longer has a father ;*

and she then touches on one of her own recurrent themes :

> et le jour n'est pas loin
> Qui de ma mort encor doit le rendre témoin.

> *and the day is not far off*
> *Which must make him witness of my death.*

Hippolyte takes this simply as meaning 'I am no longer young, and must in due course die'. But the audience knows that Phèdre has seen her death as imminent and necessary from the beginning of the play. She returns to her maternal preoccupation :

> Déjà mille ennemis attaquent son enfance.
> Vous seul pouvez contre eux embrasser sa défense.

> *Already a thousand enemies assail his childhood.*
> *You alone can take up his defence against them.*

Then the note changes, because she is moving towards her obsession :

> Mais un secret remords agite mes esprits.
> Je crains d'avoir fermé votre oreille à ses cris.
> Je tremble que sur lui votre juste colère
> Ne poursuive bientôt une odieuse mère.

> *But a secret remorse disturbs my mind.*
> *I fear that I have closed your ear to his cries.*
> *I tremble that your just anger may, falling on him,*
> *Soon revenge you on his hateful mother.*

Explicitly she refers to her earlier apparent persecution of Hippolyte, which he is now in a position to revenge. But at a deeper level, she refers to other shames. The word *odieuse* is self-punishing. Hippolyte replies frankly and truthfully :

> *Hippolyte:* Madame, je n'ai point des sentiments si bas.

> *Madame, I have no such base feelings.*

though the fuller truth is that he doesn't want to be bothered with her and her son, and wants to get away. But Phèdre goes on, now irreversibly on the other track :

> *Phèdre:* Quand vous me haïriez, je ne me plaindrais pas,
> Seigneur. Vous m'avez vue attachée à vous nuire;

100

If you were to hate me, I would not complain,
My lord. You have seen me determined to harm you;

We have had *attachée* earlier (see p. 196); it represents a savage beast on the back of its prey. It is a first note, presaging what is to follow. Her obsession with harming him was a morbid expression of her love. A hint of this escapes her :

Dans le fond de mon coeur vous ne pouviez pas lire.

You could not read in the depth of my heart.

She pulls herself back at once (if indeed she is unconscious of the slip—Hippolyte is not) :

A votre inimitié j'ai pris soin de m'offrir.
Aux bords que j'habitais je n'ai pu vous souffrir.

I took care to incur your dislike.
I could not bear to have you live where I lived.

She recounts her past enmity, obsessed with her obsession :

En public, en secret, contre vous déclarée,
J'ai voulu par des mers en être séparée ;
J'ai même défendu, par une expresse loi,
Qu'on osât prononcer votre nom devant moi.

In public, in secret, openly hostile to you,
I wanted to have the seas between us;
I even made it a strict decree
That no-one should dare speak your name in my presence.

The irony is obvious. Again she begins to lose control. She yearns towards him as she tells him how much (but not why) he ought to pity her :

Si pourtant à l'offense on mesure la peine,

But if the punishment is to be the equal of the sin

(and *she* knows how she has offended and how already she suffers punishment)

Si la haine peut seule attirer votre haine,
Jamais femme ne fut plus digne de pitié,
Et moins digne, Seigneur, de votre inimitié.

101

If my hate only could attract your hate,
No woman was ever more worthy of pity
And less worthy, my lord, of your hostility.

A curious, pathetic, and to a discerning listener a revealing paradox : poignant, dignified, and tender. But Hippolyte does not yet hear. It would be possible already at this point in the scene for an actor to register the embarrassment of a young man listening to what he fears may be a shaming indiscretion from an older person for whom he feels no sympathy. This would be reinforced by the curious—and to him embarrassing—maternal warmth of her speech. Certainly Hippolyte is embarrassed by the whole interview, and wants with increasing desperation to say something correct and get away. He now puts on a show of understanding just what she had always felt, and how natural it was : a complication of the irony. For Phèdre is giving herself away while trying desperately to control herself; while he is pretending to understand and overlook when he does not understand at all. The tempo increases, and the tension becomes unbearable.

He protests that he quite sees how it all was, with a succession of commonplaces about stepmothers :

> *Hippolyte:* Des droits de ses enfants une mère jalouse
> Pardonne rarement au fils d'une autre épouse.
> Madame, je le sais. Les soupçons importuns
> Sont d'un second hymen les fruits les plus communs.
> Toute autre aurait pour moi pris les mêmes ombrages,
> Et j'en aurais peut-être essuyé plus d'outrages.

> *A mother concerned for her children's rights*
> *Rarely forgives the son of a previous wife.*
> *I know it, madame. These unfortunate suspicions*
> *Are the most common fruit of a second marriage.*
> *Any other woman would have been as hostile to me,*
> *And I might have been treated even worse.*

This is almost comic. Phèdre is naturally stung at the obtuse suggestion that any stepmother would have felt the same and might even have behaved worse. She breaks into a melancholy little protest, with an access of added vigour. It is a delicate irony; and the reference to Heaven brings in a strange kind of blasphemy :

102

Phèdre: Ah ! Seigneur, que le ciel, j'ose ici l'attester,
De cette loi commune a voulu m'excepter !
Qu'un soin bien différent me trouble et me dévore !

Ah my lord, heaven is my witness
That it has exempted me from that common law!
That a very different trouble disturbs and consumes me!

That comes from the heart. It is also remarkably explicit, and is a grave indiscretion. But Hippolyte, though he could take Aricie's oblique statements in the previous scene, has no ears for Phèdre's much more direct hint. It is beautifully done : sad, a little sardonic, and in its last word, terribly in earnest. But he thinks she is merely devoured with grief or apprehension on Thésée's behalf; or fear for her son's future. His next words show this : he ploughs on, doggedly trying to bring the exchange to an end. He makes rather wild and not very heartfelt remarks about Thésée. All may yet be well, he says :

Hippolyte: Madame, il n'est pas temps de vous troubler encore.
Peut-être votre époux voit encore le jour ;
Le ciel peut à nos pleurs accorder son retour.

Madam, it is too soon to be feeling grief.
Perhaps your husband still sees the light of day;
Heaven may, in answer to our tears, permit his return.

The words are delicately flat here; they convey the mere conventionality of convention.

Neptune le protège, et ce dieu tutélaire
Ne sera pas en vain imploré par mon père.

Neptune is his protector, and as tutelary deity
Will not be invoked in vain by my father.

There is a crashing irony in the last couplet, for in due course Thésée invokes Neptune's aid in a curse on his son. It is extraordinary that Hippolyte should speak such fearful truth when he is only trying to find his way out of a painful embarrassment. Note also the subtle distancing of *votre époux* and *mon père*, two thoughts kept firmly four lines apart.

Phèdre is now greatly stirred. Thésée's death means that she may be free to love Hippolyte. She could not bear to think of her husband coming back, to make her once more an incestuous adulteress in thought. She speaks with energy : and can hardly help seeming to wish that Thésée should be dead, and stay dead :

> *Phèdre:* On ne voit point deux fois le rivage des morts,
> Seigneur. Puisque Thésée a vu les sombres bords,
> En vain vous espérez qu'un Dieu vous le renvoie;
> Et l'avare Achéron ne lâche point sa proie.
>
> *No man sees twice the shores of death,*
> *My lord. Since Thésée has seen those dark banks,*
> *It is in vain that you hope a god will return him to you;*
> *And the miserly Acheron never releases its prey.*

Vous espérez she says, and *vous le renvoie.* She has no such hope herself : just the reverse. Her agitation now spills over into a grave slip, a psychopathological shift of focus :

> Que dis-je? Il n'est point mort, puisqu'il respire en vous.
> Toujours devant mes yeux je crois voir mon époux.
> Je le vois, je lui parle; et mon coeur . . .
>
> *What am I saying? He is not dead, since he breathes in you.*
> *I still seem to see my husband before my eyes.*
> *I see him, speak to him; and my heart . . .*

We are reminded of a previous line, where the image of Hippolyte had pursued Phèdre so terribly (p. 192). Now, wishing to be assured that Thésée is dead, and gazing at his son, the same effect follows; the family resemblance and the obsessive passion lead her to think at one level that Thésée has come back to life, and at the deeper, truer level that she is free to love the adored son. This slips out as the beginning of a declaration of love. Horrified, she pulls herself up and makes the despairing admission :

> Je m'égare,
> Seigneur, ma folle ardeur malgré moi se déclare.
>
> *I am wandering,*
> *My lord, my mad passion declares itself despite me.*

By a humiliating irony, Hippolyte even now cannot see what is in her heart, largely because he simply does not care enough for her to pay attention. He thinks she is misled for a moment by the father-son likeness, is reminded of her loss, is pained, and is therefore behaving properly. He comes out with an almost crude and certainly cruel irony :

> *Hippolyte:* Je vois de votre amour l'effet prodigieux.

> *I see the extraordinary effect of your love.*

It is indeed; but not as he sees it :

> Tout mort qu'il est, Thésée est présent à vos yeux;
> Toujours de son amour votre âme est embrasée.

> *Dead as he is, Thésée is still before your eyes;*
> *Your spirit is still afire with his love.*

Reprieved, her lapse unnoticed, Phèdre now slips with relief into a tranced and rapturous piece of double-speaking. It turns into a direct confession :

> *Phèdre:* Oui, Prince, je languis, je brûle pour Thésée.
> Je l'aime, non point tel que l'ont vu les enfers,
> Volage adorateur de mille objets divers,
> Qui va du dieu des morts déshonorer la couche;

> *Yes Prince, I languish, I burn for Thésée.*
> *I love him, not as he was when he went down to the underworld.*
> *The fickle admirer of countless nameless women,*
> *Off to dishonour the bed of the god of the dead;*

There is a note of contempt here, and the third line suggests that Thésée is off, now, to act in death as he did in life, and even in hell to commit frivolous adultery. The note changes astonishingly as the gaze turns from inward contemplation towards the actual Hippolyte :

> Mais fidèle, mais fier, et même un peu farouche,
> Charmant, jeune, trainant tous les coeurs après soi,
> Tel qu'on dépeint nos dieux, ou tel que je vous vois.

> *But faithful, but proud, even a little timid,*
> *Charming, young, taking all hearts with him,*
> *Such as our gods are painted, or such as I see you.*

Was Thésée ever *fidèle, fier, et même un peu farouche*? Nothing leads one to believe it. Phèdre is superimposing the image of the son

105

on the memory of the father. The line, with its alliteration, its simplicity, its tenderness, is almost maternal (though *farouche* is thematic : the wild beast associated with the hunt). *Tel que je vous vois* is a direct opening of what is in her mind. Having said it, she warms to the theme, mingling recollection with desire :

> Il avait votre port, vos yeux, votre langage,
> Cette noble pudeur colorait son visage
> Lorsque de notre Crète il traversa les flots,
> Digne sujet des voeux des filles de Minos.

> *He had your bearing, your eyes, your voice,*
> *That noble shyness tinged his cheeks*
> *When he crossed the seas to our Crete,*
> *A worthy object of the love of the daughters of Minos.*

She sees that Hippolyte is pink with embarrassment, and in her affection calls it a *noble pudeur*. It is the last characteristic we associate with Thésée. It is worth dwelling a moment on Hippolyte's reactions. The first scene in the play showed us his disgust with Thésée's amours, his complicated attitude to them. When Phèdre said *Oui, Prince, je languis, je brûle pour Thésée*, the rattling l's and r's, the genuine longing in her voice (though meant for him), had the effect of reminding him of his father's ability to arouse passion in women, in her. The thought is disgusting to him; he would flinch, and show the embarrassment she now notices. The third and fourth lines are a nostalgic moment, and a moment of dynastic pride. She returns to Hippolyte; struck with a new thought, she looks more closely at him,

> Que faisiez-vous alors? Pourquoi, sans Hippolyte,
> Des héros de la Grèce assembla-t-il l'élite?

> *What were you doing then? Why did he gather together*
> *the flower of the heroes of Greece without Hippolyte?*

It is an odd suggestion. The suppressed thought behind it is that if Thésée had brought Hippolyte with him, she could have fallen in love, legitimately, with the son. She pursues, simultaneously asking and answering her question :

> Pourquoi, trop jeune encor, ne pûtes-vous alors
> Entrer dans le vaisseau qui le mit sur nos bords?

106

Too young still, why could you not
Board the vessel which took him to our shores?

She is taken with the fancy even though her own *trop jeune encor*
tells her that it is only a vain and self-deluding dream of what might
have happened. For one thing he would have been too young *for
her*; but she ignores this. Quite lost in her dream, she follows it :

Par vous aurait péri le monstre de la Crète,
Malgré tous les détours de sa vaste retraite.
Pour en développer l'embarras incertain,
Ma soeur du fil fatal eût armé votre main.

The monster of Crete would have died at your hands,
Despite the windings of its vast lair.
My sister would have furnished your hand with the fatal thread,
In order to circumvent its difficult windings.

But this puts Ariadne into too close a relationship with Hippolyte;
she dismisses the idea. If it had happened with Hippolyte instead of
with Thésée, it would have been she, Phèdre, who would have aided
him, and she says, disastrously at last, why :

Mais non, dans ce dessein je l'aurais devancée :
L'amour m'en eût d'abord inspiré la pensée.

But no, I should have outstripped her in that stratagem:
Love would have inspired the thought in me first.

And not love for Thésée, love for Hippolyte. Unconscious now of
any slip, quite carried away, she becomes explicit enough even for
Hippolyte to see her drift :

C'est moi, Prince, c'est moi dont l'utile secours
Vous eût du Labyrinthe enseigné les détours.

It is I, Prince, it is I whose useful help
Would have taught you the windings of the Labyrinth.

What extraordinary force in the bare word *utile* ! Once more Racine
shows the art of simple means (as in the rapt *C'est moi . . . c'est
moi . . .*)

Que de soins m'eût coûtés cette tête charmante !

What cares I should have spent on that beloved head!

Notice that the 'thread' used by Ariadne is abandoned. Phèdre would have taken him hand in hand into the labyrinth.

> Un fil n'eût point assez rassuré votre *amante*.

> *A thread would not have sufficed to reassure the woman who loved you.*

The word escapes her without any compunction, and she concludes in an ecstasy of retrospective wish-fulfilment :

> Compagne du péril qu'il vous fallait chercher,
> Moi-même devant vous j'aurais voulu marcher;
> Et Phèdre au Labyrinthe avec vous descendue
> Se serait avec vous retrouvée, ou perdue.

> *Companion in the peril that you had to seek out,*
> *I should have insisted on walking ahead of you myself;*
> *And Phèdre going down into the Labyrinth along with you*
> *Would have found her safety there with you, or perished with*
> *you.*

There is perhaps a characteristic touch in the *devant vous*; she is a 'forward' person. The last two lines carry overtones of their present position; are they to find themselves together, or to be lost? But *perdue* is the last word : she is now lost in two senses.

It is worth pausing a moment to survey Racine's admirable conduct of this self-disclosure. The anguished character revealing his inmost thoughts despite all conscious efforts at control is one of his principal instruments. This is the greatest of these performances; complicated by Phèdre's native dignity and self-reproach. To have worked it out in terms of this imaginary projection of the two protagonists into the past, when things might have been significantly different and happy in the outcome is an imaginative stroke of a high order. Phèdre's imagination of a joy she might have known is a piece of self-deception, as she half admits, yet it wins sympathy even as it complicates the horror of the situation.

We remember that in precisely the same way Hippolyte had realized *Je me suis engagé trop avant. Je vois que la raison cède à la violence.* He had been giving himself away to a hearer—Aricie— quick to catch every hint, because wanting to hear what he could hardly bear to admit. It is an irony that Phèdre gives herself away to a hearer who can hardly bear to be with her, and is therefore

not quick to catch her out. Thus she had dropped hints that Hippolyte had no ears for. Only now, when Phèdre has almost been forced
by his impercipience to be nakedly explicit, does he see the point.
He draws back in revulsion :

> *Hippolyte:* Dieux! qu'est-ce que j'entends? Madame, oubliez-vous
> Que Thésée est mon père, et qu'il est votre époux?

> *Gods! what do I hear? My lady, have you forgotten*
> *That Thésée is my father, and that he is your husband?*

Père and *époux* are forced into the same line by his horror. Phèdre
is stung more by the revulsion than by the justice of the observation.
She brazens it out, snapping back :

> *Phèdre:* Et sur quoi jugez-vous que j'en perds la mémoire,
> Prince? Aurais-je perdu tout le soin de ma gloire?

> *And why should you think I have forgotten it,*
> *Prince? Could I be lost to all sense of honour?*

Hippolyte is discountenanced by the angry and prompt reply. It
shows considerable if superficial self-command. In any case, he
doesn't ultimately care. He wants to get away, and apologizes for
having seen, at last, the truth, and having been horrified at it. He is
willing to say, and perhaps to believe, that he was mistaken, and
turn it into the excuse for his flight that he has been seeking all along.

> *Hippolyte:* Madame, pardonnez. J'avoue, en rougissant,
> Que j'accusais à tort un discours innocent.
> Ma honte ne peut plus soutenir votre vue;
> Et je vais ...

> *Forgive me, my lady. I confess with shame*
> *That I have put a wrong sense on an innocent declaration.*
> *I am too ashamed to remain in your presence;*
> *And I go ...*

There is something either craven or over-courtly in this. For Phèdre
the last straw is that he has understood, been horrified for a moment
and drawn away from her as from a leper, and then, because of his
fundamental indifference, adopted a front of polite excuse for his
'misunderstanding'. This is to treat her offer of love with repulsion
and then indifference. She bursts into white-hot anger, with an element
of scorn in it. You shall recognize my love, she says, monstrous

as it is: you shall not turn your face away. It is a magnificent tirade:

> *Phèdre:*   Ah! cruel, tu m'as trop entendue.
> Je t'en ai dit assez pour te tirer d'erreur.
>
>   *Ah cruel one! you understood me all too well.*
> *I have said enough to prevent any misunderstanding.*

One sees again the point of Racine's courtly language. It can be used to show many varieties of well-nuanced discourse between persons of quality; and at the last it can be dropped, so that they speak, maskless, with ferocious vigour and simplicity. The hailstorm of t's and d's here comes from bared teeth. The *tutoiement*, where before all was *Seigneur* and *Prince*, is like a blow. She exposes her madness with lucid self-hate:

> Hé bien! connais donc Phèdre et toute sa fureur.
> J'aime.
>
> *Well then! recognize Phèdre and all her madness.*
> *I am in love.*

The word is slammed out, at the beginning of the line as if she had said *je hais*. Then she turns her scorn on herself:

> Ne pense pas qu'au moment que je t'aime,
> Innocente à mes yeux, je m'approuve moi-même;
> Ni que du fol amour qui trouble ma raison
> Ma lâche complaisance ait nourri le poison.
>
> *Never think that in the moment of loving you,*
> *Innocent in my own eyes, I am content with myself;*
> *Nor that my base self-approval has fed the poison*
> *Of the mad love which clouds my reason.*

One pauses a second here. She had, earlier in the scene, done almost that. If she had not cheated her conscience, she had for a moment's fantasy laid it to sleep, and it may be the memory of this which stings her now. She had for that moment given way; and been scorned for it; so now she denies that in the long term she had ever been anything but self-observant and self-judging:

> Objet infortuné des vengeances célestes,
> Je m'abhorre encor plus que tu ne me détestes,

Luckless victim of the wrath of heaven,
I loathe myself more than you can hate me,

This is a slight change of argument; from self-judgment she turns
to herself as passive victim of a celestial plot—therefore someone to
be pitied. But in the next line she veers back to self-hatred. What
are we to make of this?

Les Dieux m'en sont témoins, ces Dieux qui dans mon flanc
Ont allumé le feu fatal à tout mon sang;
Ces Dieux qui se sont fait une gloire cruelle
De séduire le coeur d'une faible mortelle.

The gods are my witness, those gods who lit in my entrails
The fire which has been fatal to all my race;
The gods who take a cruel pride
In seducing the heart of a mere mortal woman.

The themes of external and internal responsibility are blended, in an
odd outburst. She calls the gods to witness, though they are hostile.
They relit the fires in her tainted blood (the obsessive theme of race)
and have taken evil pleasure in leading her astray. But did they? In
what way?

Then she turns on Hippolyte himself :

Toi-même en ton esprit rappelle le passé.
C'est peu de t'avoir fui, cruel, je t'ai chassé;
J'ai voulu te paraître odieuse, inhumaine;
Pour mieux te résister, j'ai recherché ta haine.

Call back the past to your own mind.
I did not merely avoid you, cruel one, I drove you away;
I tried to appear hateful and inhuman to you;
In order to resist you better, I sought your hatred.

She had hunted him like an animal after having fled him. She wanted
him to hate her so that she might the better resist him. Is this quite
truthful? She is now putting a better construction on her behaviour.

De quoi m'ont profité mes inutiles soins?
Tu me haïssais plus, je ne t'aimais pas moins.

Of what use to me were my vain endeavours?
You hated me the more, I loved you no less.

111

This is her note of anguished truth again : remarkable that the anti-thesis—a frigid device in itself—should have this pathetic effect. But the irony of events demands the ironical figure.

> Tes malheurs te prêtaient encor de nouveaux charmes.
> J'ai langui, j'ai séché, dans les feux, dans les larmes.

> *Indeed your misfortunes gave you further charms.*
> *I languished, I withered, in my fires, in my tears.*

The first line gives the faint note of sadism : to 'rejoice in the pains of the victim' would be to put it too crudely. Rather, to see with heightened acuity the attractions of the sufferer, enhanced by his suffering. But the second line is seized by the sensations; she re-enacts her own alterations of exacerbated sensation, rocking from state to state, and savouring it, with the rocking rhythm. This is much more like morbidity.

But then comes another change of mood : back to sad disenchantment :

> Il suffit de tes yeux pour t'en persuader,
> Si tes yeux un moment pouvaient me regarder.

> *You only needed to use your eyes to see it,*
> *If you could have turned your eyes on me for a moment.*

This is the truth. Hippolyte has had no eyes for her, was so indifferent to her that he could not see what others might have seen long before : never more so than in this present interview. For a moment, too, once more she asks him to look at her. He does not. It leads her to the bleakest acceptance. The tone falls :

> Que dis-je ? Cet aveu que je te viens de faire,
> Cet aveu si honteux, le crois-tu volontaire ?
> Tremblante pour un fils que je n'osais trahir,
> Je te venais prier de ne le point haïr.
> Faibles projets d'un coeur trop plein de ce qu'il aime !
> Hélas ! je ne t'ai pu parler que de toi-même.

> *What am I saying? This confession I have just made,*
> *This so shameful confession; do you think I meant to make it?*
> *Fearful for a child I could not abandon to fate,*
> *I came to beg you not to hate him.*
> *Vain purpose of a heart too full of what it loves!*
> *Alas, I could only tell you about yourself.*

112

Here she suggests the truth about her own will. Was it the gods who used her as a puppet, or was her own will the source of her actions? We need to set the *le crois-tu volontaire?* against the charge she lays above against the gods. In what sense involuntary? It is a real question.

There is a final turn. Disgusted with him, disgusted with herself, wincing with the ignominy of the whole exchange, she seeks a desperate way out. Let him kill her. Perhaps it will give them both some hint of an extreme satisfaction. The tone rises again, to frenzy :

> Venge-toi, punis-moi d'un odieux amour.
> Digne fils du héros qui t'a donné le jour,

> *Avenge yourself, punish me for my indecent love.*
> *Worthy son of the hero who engendered you,*

What tone is the reference to Thésée couched in? She starts with some violence to urge Hippolyte to take vengeance, to punish her for having offered him a disgusting love (disgusting to him only?). She lashes him with a reference to his father (a killer of monsters, certainly, but also an adulterer; nearly for once a cuckold); Hippolyte must be worthy of him. Is this a sneer? Perhaps not, but one hardly knows how to take it if it is not,

> Délivre l'univers d'un monstre qui t'irrite.
> La veuve de Thésée ose aimer Hippolyte !
> Crois-moi, ce monstre affreux ne doit point t'échapper.
> Voilà mon coeur. C'est là que ta main doit frapper.

> *Rid the universe of a monster which enrages you.*
> *The widow of Thésée dares to love Hippolyte!*
> *Ah no, the frightful monster must not escape you.*
> *Here is my heart. Here your hand must strike.*

She is now almost beside herself. The reference to the monster (one of many such references in the play) identifies her with the former Minotaur whom she would have wished to help Hippolyte slay. And if that exploit had an obscure sexuality about it, so too does her present offer. The exacerbating further reference to Thésée (towards whom Hippolyte has such complicated feelings), to herself as his widow daring to love Hippolyte, is now meant actively to excite his repulsion, as well as to wound herself. She repeats that she is a

113

monster, and must be hunted down. Having earlier offered him her love, she now bares her breast, to offer him her life.

The excited parallel is inescapable. She becomes yet more exalted, thirsting for the blow, sensing, not seeing (for she has her eyes shut), the hand reaching towards her, to pluck out her heart :

> Impatient déjà d'expier son offense,
> Au-devant de ton bras je le sens qui s'avance.

> *Already eager to expiate its sin,*
> *I can feel it [my heart] reaching out to meet your arm*

or

> *I can sense it [your hand] coming out with the force*
> *of your arm behind it.*

The one word 'Frappe' *('Strike')* at the end of this almost-ecstasy is like a plea for a sexual release. Hippolyte being by now transfixed with confusion and horror, she begs for his sword

> Ou si tu le crois indigne de tes coups,
> Si ta haine m'envie un supplice si doux
> Ou si d'un sang trop vil ta main serait trempée,
> Au défaut de ton bras prête-moi ton épée.
> Donne.

> *Or if you think it too base for your strokes,*
> *If your hatred envies me so sweet a torture,*
> *Or if your hand would be dipped in too vile a blood,*
> *Give me your sword instead of your arm [behind it],*
> *Here.*

Another single word at the end of an extended climax-like sentence, as she snatches the sword. One observes that to be killed by him is *un supplice si doux*, which is explicit enough. The thought, already perverse, is complicated by the new violence against him which makes her think his enmity would envy such a sweet fate for her, and the realism which makes her recognize that he now feels horror for her, and would think himself contaminated by her death as much as he would have been by her love—the two things being now almost one.

Oenone, too late, intervenes. Phèdre is almost insensible, on her knees, her clothes dishevelled, her eyes shut in a rapture of misery and shame, begging for the pleasure of death, his sword in her hand.

Someone is coming. She cannot be seen like this. Oenone bundles her off, in mid-rhyme :

Oenone: Que faites-vous, Madame? Justes Dieux !
Mais on vient. Evitez des témoins odieux;
Venez, rentrez, fuyez une honte certaine.

What are you doing, Madam? Just gods!
Someone is coming. Flee hateful witnesses;
Come, come inside, flee inevitable shame.

The upshot of this encounter is that Phèdre has betrayed herself in a way so utterly humiliating that it is hardly conceivable that she should ever recover her poise. One is tempted to say that she has been 'subjected' to a kind of torture and public disgrace combined. The point is, however, that everything that happens bursts out of her. These are all things she cannot prevent herself saying and doing. Hippolyte too is equally the prey of his own nature; he has just made the same kind of confession to Aricie (kindly received, as it happens) but his community of plight and experience does not in the least incline him to understand Phèdre or to sympathize with her; it is a fact of his nature that he is revolted by her, and nothing could be more distasteful to him than having her press herself upon him.

So in this long and beautifully conducted exchange we watch and listen with a mixture of horror and sympathy. The great pattern of Racine's drama, the ultimately disheartening aspect of it, is the way in which, if we listen carefully to what his people say, we do indeed learn why when *he* has just said *this*, *she* says *that*. We learn two things : what they are like and why they do what they do; and why, though we understand them, they cannot possibly understand each other : why therefore their relationships are blind and destructive. It is a demonstration, again, of the archetypal powers of drama. These people, merely speaking, create themselves in our presence and our hearing. They come into focus, and acquire dimensions. We see into them as they disclose themselves, in a way that we do not see into other people in life. Yet the clairvoyance *we* are given is denied *them*; they cannot understand or forgive each other, and they bring each other down. Their tragedy is that of the individual will locked into its cell of selfhood; seeing and hearing through the distorting medium of that selfhood, and for lack of transcendence condemned

115

to destructive assaults on others : assaults which are themselves blind and self-defeating. It is a terrible world.

That is the moral substance of Racine's greatest play. The basic idea is that the human animal is rather like a hermit crab. It is a tender shrinking creature armoured by a thick carapace of selfhood into which it can retire, but which is a burden and a hindrance and ultimately makes the inhabitant vulnerable to any shrewd enemy which can get a weapon into the opening of the shell.

The actual master-images of the play form a kind of psychological cluster which can be, to some extent, teased out and displayed analytically. Racine took his mythology very seriously. It was not just a source of atmosphere or background but of meanings, so that the constant stream of allusions builds up into a structure.

Phèdre was the daughter of Minos, king of Crete, the island where the Minotaur, at the centre of the labyrinth, received every nine years a blood-tribute of male and female virgins, until Theseus, guided through the labyrinth by holding a thread whose other end was held by Ariadne, killed the monster.

Phèdre's ancestry is charged with strange elements. Her father Minos was son of Zeus and Europa and was associated with the kingdom of the dead; her mother Pasiphaë was a daughter of the sun-god, was impregnated by a god-sent bull, and was in fact the mother of the Minotaur, who was therefore Phèdre's half-brother. Theseus killed this monster, and she thereafter married Theseus.

One French word for heredity, as in English, is 'blood', *sang*. The monster demanded an annual blood-sacrifice, but in the end Theseus shed *its* blood. The old legend begins to set up relationships in which tainted heredity, bloodshed and monstrosity are dominant elements. So is the idea of the labyrinth : a winding recess in which there lurks a monster who will kill you, or who must be killed. You are its prey, in a regular sacrifice, if you are a virgin or youth.

Hippolyte is a virgin who is in the end sacrificed to another monster, sent by Neptune because Thésée has cursed him and invoked the god's aid in fulfilling the curse. Hippolyte is a hunter and horseman, associated persistently with Diana-images : the free wild young beasts of the forest, who are the prey of various predators, including man, and may become stricken deer. The central image, blood, links these themes of tainted ancestry, sacrifice, hunting, virginity. An

116

associated image is the darkness of the forest (in which hunters and hunted move freely) and the darkness of the labyrinth, where a narrow twisting corridor leads to a fatal encounter. These two darknesses contrast with the other master image, light. The original Greek name, Phaedra, means 'light-bringer'. Light is derived from the ancestral sun god; morally, it is the light of justice and goodness which falls on things polluted. It does not penetrate the forest (which can be a cool retreat from detection) or the labyrinth (which is a place where one is lost, kills, or is killed).

There are other elements; while the blood may be tainted by an ancestral fate or curse, it may also be fired with disease. A perverse or guilty love is therefore naturally figured as a disease of the blood. A virgin young man whom you love in a guilty way, is quickly associated with the free young animals he hunts; therefore a dominating love would tame him, break him in. A disastrously guilty love would turn him into a sacrificial victim, if his blood were shed. And this happens.

These resonances in the play are not merely announced, or merely exchanged. They have an active interplay with each other which builds up into a network of motives which are mutually modified and enriched. It is a property of language that words have 'semantic fields', areas of overlapping meanings where one word calls up, naturally enough, another which is a near-synonym. But that is a very simple operation : words also call up their opposites, by a natural reversal-process. They also call up words which are associated in much more complex associative ways.

Racine sets up associations within this play which operate for the play alone. So the word 'forest' acquires the sense of coolness and retreat and darkness, naturally enough. And this associates, by reversal, with 'light'. But in the play there are added overtones about guilt and innocence, which are enforced by the context. The inhabitants of the forest, hunters and hunted, are linked in a natural association. The qualification of virginity is perhaps a natural mythological association with Diana as huntress. The idea that the animals may be caught and tamed, or sacrificed, is a natural extension. The idea that Hippolyte, the hunter, is himself such an animal is so to speak 'induced' by the context. So is the idea that the stricken deer, hit by the huntsman's arrow, trails a scent of shed blood; that this attracts a ravenous beast of prey which leaps on to its back and drags it down. But the play induces the idea that this beast attracted by blood is the goddess of love (*Vénus toute entière à sa proie attachée*); and by a cinematic shift this becomes a figure of Phèdre herself.

I need again to say that these correspondences are not neat equivalences. In Racine, as in Shakespeare, this is not an algebra of motives in which figure 1 always equals meaning 1. I am suggesting instead that the figures move in and out of relationship with each other, producing something like harmonic mutations of each other. There are large domains of conceptual force, governed by the key words *sang, lumière, monstre* and so on. But these are not unchanging and neatly mapped.

Once again one thinks of Wagner, of course. He has been subjected to much boring analysis of his motives. Indeed he invited it, and one must concede that some of his motives *are* inert, and one rather shrinks from the recurrences. In the *Ring*, if someone talks of a sword, we shall hear a musical sword, and the musical phrase does nothing for the idea. But at his finest the correspondences that Wagner sets up are an invitation to enter a real psychic depth which can be best felt and explored, not paraphrased in words.

I am suggesting that Racine too is doing something of this kind. When Phèdre in an agony of envy envisages Hippolyte and Aricie enjoying a love which is all that hers is not—innocent, mutual, self-approved—she launches into a music which is ostensibly simple but enriched with the meanings Racine has been building up :

> Les a-t-on vus souvent se parler, se chercher?
> Dans le fond des forêts allaient-ils se cacher?
> Hélas ! Ils se voyaient avec pleine licence;
> Le ciel de leurs soupirs approuvait l'innocence;
> Ils suivaient sans remords leur penchant amoureux,
> Tous les jours se levaient clairs et sereins pour eux.

> *Have they been often seen, talking, looking for each other?*
> *Did they go off to hide themselves in the depth of the forest?*
> *Alas! They saw each other in complete liberty!*
> *Heaven approved the innocence of their vows;*
> *They followed without remorse their loving feeling,*
> *Every day dawned clear and serene for them.*

The master image of the play is given a momentary kindliness; for once the light is warm and clear rather than pitiless or sullied. She goes on

118

Et moi, triste rebut de la nature entière,
Je me cachais au jour, je fuyais la lumière ...

And I, sad reject of the whole of nature,
I hid myself from the day, I fled the light ...

(like Cain or a scapegoat; like the monster in the labyrinth). This
links with her very last words :

Déjà je ne vois plus qu' à travers un nuage
Et le ciel et l'époux que ma présence outrage ;
Et la mort à mes yeux dérobant la clarté
Rend au jour qu'ils souillaient toute sa pureté.

Already I can only see through a cloud
The heaven and the husband who are outraged by my existence;
And death, removing illumination from my eyes
Restores all its purity to the day they sullied.

The clouded vision is an obvious and striking irony; it had been
clouded all through life. But the simple figure is marvellously enriched in the last two lines. The film over the eye is transferred to
the eye of day itself; it was she who polluted the light, and her death
vindicates her ancestor and restores its purity. With that word, the
impossible ideal, on her lips, she dies.

One might also point out that at some moment in the play everyone is called a 'monster' : Phèdre sees even Hippolyte as a monster.
The monster in us which bursts out and does things which amaze
even us, since we had not known what we are capable of, this is one
of the themes of the play, reinforced by the patterned action in which
the main characters are consistently unable to stop themselves doing
something disastrous. The monster in the labyrinth, one might too
neatly but not inappropriately say, is the irreducible self at the end
of the recesses of personality. Since it turns out that in Racine's
world we prey on the people we love, the Minotaur also figures the
loved one whom in the end we destroy or are destroyed by. Pressing
for meanings of the play, we come out with these equations. They
are not exactly false : something like that is implied. But Racine
is not using his mythology to provide him with neat flat allegorical
meanings, obvious morals, or even psychological theories. He is producing what one can hardly avoid calling a music of themes, which
develop, harmonize, clash, build up or dissolve. They are carrying a

meaning which is meant to be felt, not paraphrased; and in this respect too dramatic poetry is like music.

I have been reluctant to press too much French on the reader who may not read it easily. I have placed in a long appendix a detailed study of Racine's verse which moves from the basic form of the Alexandrine to consider the musical uses to which it was put (once again the analogy is useful) and considers also the fine structure of the verbal texture. It is not possible to say anything specific about any poetic drama without making direct contact of that sort with the words : indeed the only alternative is to fall into the stereotypes about classical tragedy which only the words themselves can show to be false.

I do find myself saying, however, that the texture of this verse, much subtler than is generally allowed, is nonetheless distinctly less dense, rich and full than Shakespeare's. This is a matter of the local metaphoric life, which has in Shakespeare such an extraordinary and constantly surprising inventiveness : which does not, paradoxically, strike us as Shakespeare's inventiveness, but as the character's self, in an immediacy which has a living texture laid bare in more layers than Racine's. It is not a question of a self-advertising 'medium', still less of poetic 'ornamentation'. The language is inseparable from the revelation it mediates. A part of the authenticity of Shakespeare's insight is the actual element of gratuitousness, unpredictability, refusal to be schematically systematic. Racine's motivic structure in *Phèdre* is more grand and symmetrical in outline than anything in Shakespeare : looks more planned, is in detail more neat. This has something to do with its being derived from a mythology—which is not, in the end, Racine's own system of beliefs, however marvellously he has given it life. It has a good deal also to do with a language which is ceasing to be popular—losing contact with the vigour of spontaneous utterance by the generality of human beings speaking their life and their nature directly, so that the heart moves into the mouth.

7

A Note on Spanish Drama

The period of Spanish world dominance preceded that of France. In what the British think of as the 'Elizabethan' period Spain was an Imperial power : the leading European state, with a proud history of having thrown back the incursion of Islam, of having been the frontier-defender of Christendom. Spanish monarchs now ascended as if by right the throne of the Holy Roman Empire, and by a natural consequence Spain ceased to be a frontier nation and dominated the heartlands of Europe. Much of Italy, the Netherlands, of Germany and Austria fell under Spanish or related Habsburg rule. The importance for us is that these countries became channels of Spanish culture. Through Naples, through independent Venice in the south, through the equally important trading cities in the Netherlands, passed an artistic trade : specifically troupes of actors, adaptors, translators, theorists, of the drama.

In Europe today Spanish is not known and read as it once was, so it is as if an important and characteristic voice has fallen silent. It is known, in general terms, that renaissance Spain had a golden age, and that this produced a great literature, including a great drama. But this is taken, once more, to be something on the periphery. Yet it is a central strand in the development of European culture : especially in the drama. I cannot press on the reader with no Spanish long quotations which will give him the flavour of this drama. The output of plays was in any case so enormous—far larger than in England or indeed than the whole of the rest of Europe put together—that a few samples would be pointless. I can in this brief Note only indicate that a mental place has, so to speak, to be reserved, a large area in the historical consciousness.

The active period of Spanish drama begins even earlier than the English and goes on as long as the French, and is continuous in a way that the English and French were not. That is to say, if you mark a period of maturity as beginning in England and Spain in about 1570–1590, in England this is interrupted by the Civil War, and after the reopening of the theatres English drama has perceptibly changed—partly because the theatres are now more like modern theatre buildings, partly because the audience was in consequence a different one, partly because times had changed, and the language with them. It was at this period—roughly 1660 onwards—that the French theatre 'took off' and had its brief but enormously influential flowering. But the greatest Spanish dramatist, Calderón, did not die until 1681, and the theatres he was writing for were like those of a hundred years before. Indeed the *corrales* of Madrid were to an uncanny degree like the theatres of Elizabethan England, and they remained basically unchanged until the 1730s or 1740s. They were open or courtyard theatres, without lighting, played in the daylight and with no performances when it rained. As in England, the entrance charge was low, and the audience popular. The later reconstruction of Spanish theatres was directly connected with the transition from a traditional popular and national theatre to an aristocratic or courtly theatre associated with the cult of opera and of translated 'classical' drama, or the attempts of Spanish dramatists, long after the genuinely classical period of the national culture, to produce a neo-classical art based on foreign—specifically French—models.

The descriptive categories I have applied to English drama apply equally to Spanish : it was popular, national, conventional, in verse. More : it was religious, or one whole element of it was. The characteristic form of the *auto*, cultivated especially by Calderón in the last 30 years of his long and productive life, was an allegorical religious drama appealing directly to the popular religious sense. It was in some ways a prolongation of medieval drama : the *auto* was staged in the open on four carts until 1705. Suppressed for political-cultural reasons in 1765, *autos* went on being performed in the villages until the nineteenth century : an amazing example of the toughness and tenacity of an artistic form which appealed deeply to the communal consciousness.

In the second quarter of the seventeenth century, which the English naturally think of as the immediate aftermath of Shakespeare, Europeans were conscious that the drama of the dominant nation, Spain, and the dominant language, Spanish, was the drama which formed taste. They would find themselves, however, confronting a drama which did not translate well, for the reasons which prevent any poetic drama translating well. The Spanish drama is 'in' the poetry in the same way as Shakespeare's is : rather more so in the sense that Spanish verse-forms are very intricate and varied. A certain amount, however, *would* translate. Spanish plots are full of movement and change, like the English ones : there are similar demands on the imagination of the audience, which has to accept rapid changes of locale and a fluid time-scheme. There is also much straightforward physical movement in a theatre which displays the passions in action, not merely in utterance. There are, especially, theatricalities of gesture : especially those gestures of the hand which express friendship, love, seduction, defiance, alliance, forgiveness, deception, invocation, cursing, benediction and so on; also tableau-like effects (especially expressive forms of kneeling).

This characteristic energy gives a peculiar kind of audience-involvement; and the poetic utterance furthers it. It is fair to say however that the Spanish drama was not as 'inward' as Shakespeare or Racine, because the poetry is of a different kind. The sense of characterisation is therefore different. Nothing in Spanish drama offers the equivalent of Hamlet, Macbeth, Othello, or Racine's fierce women : Phèdre, Hermione, Athalie. The actual situation of Othello recurs very often : the married nobleman who knows or fears that his honour has been injured by a slight or an infidelity. What in those circumstances is a man of honour to do? It is argued in those terms : the honour concerned is almost an external thing like a coat of arms, and the drama comes from the conflict between an external social demand and an answering social responsibility fought out in a man who also has personal feelings. This is quite unlike Othello, who is at the end of the play lost in his private world of obsessions. It is a basic element of Shakespeare's play that Desdemona is entirely innocent.

The poetry of such a self-expression was bound to be different, especially in a country where the reaffirmed domination of the Counter-Reformation Church meant that debate on these issues had to be conducted with at least one eye on the orthodox ruling. Duelling and secret marriages were matters on which the Church had pronounced : they were also staple situations in drama. The bold bad man of the universal popular theatre had to be related in Spain more closely to the universal salvific will of God : God could redeem such people and demonstrate the sovereignty of his will and the extraordinariness of his mercy. Tirso de Molina's Don Juan is not damned by 'negative antecedent reprobation' but through the identifiable misuse of his free will. He goes down to hell to demonstrate the fallacy of Lutheran belief—the arrogant faith in God's pardon which enables one to sin boldly. The popular stage was thus a kind of wayside pulpit as well as a popular debating chamber for the representation of national myths and the exploration of current social concerns : personal worth and honour, the true road to salvation, the moral and legal basis of kingship, the destructiveness of unsanctioned sexuality. Hence, of course, some opposition from the Church, which saw its role encroached upon.

In these circumstances a dramatist may escape a full and damaging self-commitment by staging a *debate*, in which the characters are mouth-pieces for a point of view, rather than fully dramatized personalities like Othello. And indeed the Spanish drama does, in general, tend rather to take this form—as did Corneille's drama, much influenced by Spanish models. The characters act out a tension, which is centred in the protagonist. He is indeed torn, but the things which tear him are certainly not private, and almost not personal. The poetry rather tends to be handed round the characters impartially, and not to convey 'character'. The point at which this kind of drama becomes peculiarly interesting is where a protagonist in some difficult set of circumstances resorts to the extremely conventional, indeed universal, renaissance theatrical device of adopting a disguise. He steps in and out of social and sexual identities in order to prevail against them. This produces a specific dynamism of the individual will, meaning to survive and prevail. A conscious intelligence has to dominate its own native impulsions. The adoption of another identity produces this kind of tension, of which the character is conscious, and which he shares with the audience. This is a kind of 'interiority'. But because the splitting is a willed process, and the will remains dominant, it is not a morbid state. Once again, we are on the way to Corneille.

This rather conscious, somewhat olympian attitude can only be conveyed by an even more olympian playwright, who is working out this dialectic between characters who are not allowed to run away with the piece; to take the whole drama into themselves. This can produce poetic structures of impressive complexity. Professor Sullivan shows how Tirso uses 'base' images which can be extended by developing the field : by double meanings, ambiguities, image clusters. His *La Venganza de Tamar* takes the Old Testament story in which Amnon rapes his sister. The base images are derived from the story itself : blood, eating, and flowers. The 'blood' relationship is basic, and Racine's use of it in *Phèdre* is very similar. Amnon feigns illness and lack of appetite to bring Tamar to him, and is finally slain at a banquet. The associations with 'appetite'—being starving, being unwilling to eat, being ravenous—quickly convert to sexual analogues. Tamar's defloration links flowers and blood in images which go back to the oldest taboos, and open out into other images. Hints of cannibalism, of the sacrament, of sacred prostitution or the incestuous linkings of gods lurk in the background, and make this a curiously disturbing play.

The Spanish play which came to represent the greatness of the whole tradition is Calderón's *La vida es sueño*, a play of European importance : in itself, and because it was admired, acted, adapted, translated throughout the continent. It prompts comparison with Sophocles in a way no other European play can match, because it stems from the same kind of mythic paradox. A king, warned by an oracle that his son will supplant him, prevents fate by having the son immured in a tower, where he grows up a savage. Released by a series of chances, he does indeed overthrow his father momentarily, only to prove himself more magnanimous than his father. The savage son, Segismundo, undergoes tests and traumas which convince him that life is, in various senses, a dream. He ends the play as wise as dreaming men can be. The notion of fatality, of free will, of the personal fatedness inherent in personality, the strange but simple force of the action, and the gravity of the moralizing make it a unique play with a parabolic force like that of *Oedipus* and *Lear* and the Book of Job. It manages to be both very simple in an age-old way, and endlessly reverberant. It is in touch with the roots of the folk in the way that ballads, romances, folktales and fairy stories are.

It was this that ultimately appealed in later centuries. The importance of Spanish drama in later European literary history is that when the neo-classical blight settled on the theatre, and when by a rather perverse mischance Racine was presented as its ancestor, Calderón could be called up alongside Shakespeare as an equal power in another native tradition. The new internationalism in art (*afrancesamiento* was the Spanish word for 'frenchification') was countered by appealing to the force of two national theatres : the English and the Spanish. These, being national and popular, were now thought of as 'romantic'. Their example laid on romantic dramatists the obligation, first of all in Germany, to found a national drama which would also be 'romantic'. It would not fear to deal with national history; it would strive to be authentically national, even folkloric, in costume and setting; it would be freer in its utterance than conventional classical drama; it would be in verse. Whether it would be 'poetic' is another matter. This was partly something to do with the state of the language : it was also something to do with the inwardness of the drama, and the ability therefore to give the characters an idiom in which the 'will' could be directly expressed.

8

Poetic Drama
and Neo-classicism

I have been trying to present a commonplace of literary history in a
way which makes it real, specific, and felt. Everyone knows that the
century and a half from 1550 (say) to 1700 or just before was the
great age of European drama, with its three great national traditions :
Spanish, English, French. Each national tradition is rooted in a
medieval popular tradition which had once been more international
because ultimately derived from the festivals of the Church. In the
early modern period these traditions identified themselves *as* national.
English and Spanish drama came to maturity first, and the forms
remained popular in ways I have pointed towards. In France, in the
1660s and 1670s, the drama assumed a crucially important classical
form in which it lost its popular nature. This was partly a matter of
subject and external forms, much more a matter of language. However, even in French classical tragedy a fundamental convention of
non-naturalistic form remained : the use of verse. And in Racine's
hands the verse was such, the language was such, that the drama was
still, as for Shakespeare, an interior drama in the sense I have tried
to define; it was therefore a matter of 'character' in the sense I have
also tried to define : character being not just an aggregation of visible
characteristics ('traits of character' or even 'quirks of character') but
a matter of revealing a deep inner nature and letting the spectator
feel it so directly that he is in danger of identifying himself with it.
This is because really to grasp the whole force of the poetic utterance
is necessarily to move inside the character's skin and to feel with his
feelings, which immediately become his words. In this way Racine's
drama, more than Calderón's or Lope's, is like Shakespeare's.

The national traditions thus have affinities. Spanish is popular,
vernacular, national and formally free, like the English. The French

(in Racine) is internal, like Shakespeare's. The English drama has resemblances both with its contemporary in Spain and its successor in France. The one thing they all share is the use of a poetic medium which is primary and constitutive. It supports the other conventions of speech, especially of monologue (aside, soliloquy, tirade) which permit a character to reveal to an audience what is passing within him.

The natural and habitual use of verse gives what is spoken by all the characters in a play a certain homogeneity, as of a family-likeness. Fundamental to the traditions is a use of metaphor which not only provides the inwardness with Macbeth's or Othello's perceptions, emotions and nature : it can link Macbeth and Lady Macbeth morally because it links them poetically : so also with Othello and Iago. It can be therefore a structural device; it develops as in a symphonic music of motives into a continuum which not only joins one item temporally and sequentially to the next but develops into a structure of effects which are perceived in relationship and cohere as a whole. There is a letter which may be by Mozart or not, but if he did not say this, he could have :

> The thing becomes finished in the head—although it may be long —so that I can afterwards embrace it in the mind, so to speak, with one look, like a beautiful picture; and I hear it in my imagination not successively as it must be heard later on, but somehow all together.

Shakespeare, Jonson, Lope, Tirso, Calderón, Racine powerfully, Corneille less powerfully, all these playwrights produce that kind of structure by using verse.

In any language it is only by the use of metaphor, and especially by approaching Shakespeare's extraordinarily concerted use of it, that a direct sense of the 'movement of the will' can be given. The image-clusters and image-chains which are generated in that use of language simultaneously become a structural element of the play. The characters who in duets or ensembles develop variations or extensions of basic images show their nature, their kinship with each other, and also elaborate a 'meaning' for the play, which becomes more than the simple interchange of neutral speech, or the simple interaction of externally presented *personae*. The play is not just what they say and do, what happens; it is its meaning when it is 'embraced

128

in the mind' or heard in the imagination 'not successively . . . but all together.' The structure of effects so subtly and multifariously built up is primarily *felt*, not just heard. Or if it is heard as sounds, as words, it instantaneously resolves and spreads into a tissue of feelings which are not entirely verbal. No verbal equivalent (other than the play itself, performed by the reader in his head, or performed by actors and watched by an audience) can, by paraphrase, do anything but denature and reduce the effect : which is why analyses like mine, useful so far as they go, are only a kind of passport which is best thrown away as soon as you feel you are over the border and into the world of feeling of the play.

I am of course talking about an organic art-form, of the kind desiderated by critics since Lessing, and especially the great romantic critics. The musical analogy presses itself on us again : the verse-form of this poetic drama does seem like an early analogue of the mature music-drama of Wagner or Verdi, where the unifying structural principle is a continuous musical medium. One can even say without straining the analogy too much that the early disjunction between relatively flat dialogue and the great set-piece speech (as in Marlowe) is not unlike the disjunction between dry recitative and formal aria; while Shakespeare's and Racine's more through-composed drama, when even the small 'functional' exchanges are soaked in and contribute to the motivic texture, is like the continuous music of the great masters.

True enough, but it remains a rather willed and superficial analogy between forms. The more fundamental analogy is between objectives — the one about the movement of the will which I have often touched on, and a deeper one about ways of meaning. A characteristic of ordinary daily language is its redundancy : an ill-apprehended meaning is conveyed by repetition or variation which makes up for being merely approximate by smothering the target. This is as much as to say that anything can be rephrased, and usually is. I can convey a rough meaning in these words, or in almost entirely other words. I paraphrase myself; you see what, more or less, I mean (I have just done it.) The point about metaphorical language is that the charge it conveys is not a propositional meaning : it is a set of effects. These effects can be conveyed no other way. Paraphrase of metaphor may be explanation of the broad meaning, it is not identity of effect. In this respect the effect of metaphor is like a musical effect.

129

It was a commonplace in the eighteenth century to say that the effect of music could not be put into words because it was 'too vague'. Words, it was thought, conveyed like impressions to you and me, since we are both rational, and human nature is the same, and the associational process is limited and understood, and mostly blocked off by propositional utterances. We know what we want to say, say it, and are understood. If language works like that, music, which does not work like that, is 'vague' because it is entirely unpropositional, and more associative.

The train of thought was reversed in the nineteenth century: for instance by Mendelssohn. Writing to Marc André Souchay who had asked him the 'meaning' of his 'songs without words' (a provocative title), Mendelssohn replied

> There is so much talk about music, and yet so little is said. For my part, I believe that words do not suffice for such a purpose, and if I found they did suffice I would finally have nothing more to do with music. People often complain that music is too ambiguous; that what they should think when they hear it is so unclear, whereas everyone understands words. With me it is exactly the reverse, and not only with regard to an entire speech, but also with individual words. These too seem to me so ambiguous, so vague, so easily misunderstood in comparison to genuine music, which fills the soul with a thousand things better than words. The thoughts which are expressed to me by music that I love are not too indefinite to be put into words, but on the contrary, too definite. And so I find in every effort to express such thoughts, that something is right but at the same time that something is lacking in all of them; and so I feel, too, with yours. This however, is not your fault, but the fault of the words which are incapable of anything better. If you ask me what I was thinking when I wrote it, I would say : just the song as it stands. And if I happen to have had certain words in mind for one or other of these songs, I would never want to tell them to anyone because the same words can never mean the same things to different people. Only the song can say the same thing, can arouse the same feelings in one person as in another, a feeling which is not expressed however by the same words.

A number of points are conflated here. Mendelssohn's final claim for music is rather like Schopenhauer's, but not identical. It is in fact untrue, or at any rate undiscoverable or unprovable, that the same piece of music produces 'the same feelings in one person as another'. This sort of absolutist claim could also be made for poetry (poetic drama for instance), or more obviously for painting, sculpture or expressive gesture, which do not use words either. The fundamental truth that Mendelssohn conveys is that low-level verbal communication can be paraphrased without loss because the meanings are conventional or approximate. Poetry, though it is in words, can be no more paraphrased than music, and this because the impact of a given deliberate collocation of words in poetry is not primarily propositional but meant to be felt as a tissue of effects, passing from the verbal one into other ways of feeling the words. A precisely considered effect (or, if you like, an absolutely precise meaning) is not paraphrasable, any more than music is. The metaphors in Shakespeare and Racine are of this kind, since although a verbal analysis can point to the effects, it does not produce them. So with music criticism, which Mendelssohn almost rules out of court as a possibility while also making it unnecessary. For if we did all feel music in exactly the same way we should not need to try to improve our grasp of it, or offer to do so for others. The justice of his position is that the best kind of practical criticism of music, as of poetry, is a deeply considered performance which is as deeply apprehended, and so escapes the approximations and deformations of paraphrase, commentary or analysis.

The same dissatisfaction with the inadequacies of ordinary language and conventional thought about it, animated the great romantic literary critics. In English literature it was Coleridge who sketched out the new poetics of organic form, as in this passage, claiming

> . . . that Poetry, even that of the loftiest and, seemingly, that of the wildest Odes, had a logic of its own, as severe as that of science, and more difficult, because more subtle, more complex, and dependent on more, and more fugitive causes. In the truly great poets . . . there is a reason assignable, not only for every word, but for the position of every word.

That is, the words are not units, like bricks in a wall or knots on a string : they are part of a tissue which is not just a syntactic structure, or an equation where a set of words in an agreed order equals a proposition, a meaning. They have, instead of a mere meaning, a complex effect. Partly this is secured rhythmically, partly by tone or melody, partly by association (which is like a harmonic effect added to a melodic one). The 'logic' Coleridge is talking about is not therefore the logic of philosophers—who have an artificial language, a symbolic logic, in which propositions are conveyed and tested for truth-conditions, consistency, logical dependence. It is the 'logic' of the mind, which is quicker and more comprehensive than the other sort, and often 'illogical' by its standards. It slips across rational chasms on the tightrope of association; its 'inductions' are more like those of electricity. The reader who grants my analysis of Othello's language (therefore of Othello's mind) will see that it can be the tortured logic of obsession, which is certainly 'irrational' while also comprehensible. As friend of Othello you would want to try to argue him out of his illogic, while recognizing the futility of the attempt, and the awful logic in his associations. As spectator, one is spellbound by Shakespeare's gift, which is simultaneously dramatic, poetic, and psychological. One is differently impressed by the imaginative power —also a verbal power—with which Racine in *Phèdre* cumulatively works out the shadowy associations of image-clusters which he has derived from classical myth : an instrument which enables him too to explore psychic depths in characters who are related to each other in this way and yet remain distinct.

In modern technical terms these poetic plays are indeed systems of signs. They transcend that kind of structuralist terminology by being more complex than most structuralists allow. The signs are not, for instance, arbitrary, as the signs in an algebra are, or the signs in a natural language are said to be (they aren't, mostly, or rapidly cease to be so). These signs are derived from a practical psychology which is laden with natural associations, or from a mythology which is crusted with centuries of accreted meaning. They have natural and profound suggestive force which may not be universal but is certainly widely shared by people within the culture. The interrelationship of the signs within the system of the play almost automatically starts to build up and deepen the associations, the meanings, and to develop them in the sense needed by the play itself.

This systematic aspect was also well understood by Coleridge :

> But if the definition sought for be that of a *legitimate* poem, I answer it must be one, the parts of which mutually support and explain each other; all in their proportion harmonizing with and

supporting the purpose and known influences of metrical arrangement. The philosophic critics of all ages coincide with the ultimate judgement of all countries, in equally denying the praises of a just poem, on the one hand, to a series of striking lines or distiches, each of which, absorbing the whole attention of the reader to itself, disjoins it from its context, and makes it a separate whole, instead of a harmonizing part; and on the other hand, to an unsustained composition, from which the reader collects rapidly the general result, unattracted by the component parts.

It is no accident that Coleridge stands in that succession—that European tradition of his time—of critics who re-educated readers who had accepted the commonplace judgement that Shakespeare was a barbarian of intuitive genius, who produced flashes of insight, gems of poetry and snatches of music in an art that was ultimately formless—that he was, in a word, artless. Coleridge, like Lessing and the Schlegels, retorted—and Coleridge and A. W. Schlegel actually demonstrated—that Shakespeare was a conscious artist whose every effect was intended and would be considered deeply calculated if we did not have the counter-impression that he was miraculously spontaneous, or at any rate swift in the way that Mozart was swift. As A. W. Schlegel said :

> The activity of genius is, it is true, natural to it, and, in a certain sense, unconscious; and consequently the person who possesses it is not always at the moment able to render an account of the course which he may have pursued; but it by no means follows, that the thinking power had not a great share in it. It is from the very rapidity and certainty of the mental process, from the utmost clearness of understanding, that thinking in a poet is not perceived as something abstracted, does not wear the appearance of reflex meditation. That notion of poetical inspiration which many lyrical poets have brought into circulation . . . is least of all applicable to dramatic composition, one of the most thoughtful productions of the human mind. It is admitted that Shakespeare has reflected, and deeply reflected, on character and passion, on the progress of events and human destinies, on the human constitution, on all the things and relations of the world . . . So that it was only for the structure of his own pieces that he had no thought to spare?

It may seem to us strange that this had to be said; that it had to be repeated for many years, at first by people who were conscious

133

that the idea would strike hearers as strange, or even ridiculous. We have no useful comment on the essential nature of poetic drama from Shakespeare's own time, apart from occasional shrewd comments or parodies in the drama itself. Did Shakespeare's audiences have a concept of 'organic form'? Almost certainly not. It is a reasonable assumption that Shakespeare had one, since his plays have the form they do : but he would not have needed to elaborate the idea as a consciously held concept, since it was sufficient to write the plays as examples. It is a mystery that readers and playgoers had by 1700 so distanced themselves from Shakespeare that they had to begin to make excuses for him, or extenuate his drama on the ground that he wrote in a barbaric age.

The English themselves never lost all sense of his greatness : in one way or another he went on being 'revived' in the English theatre in the eighteenth century by great actors; and, well acted, he went on making his stage effect. Readers, however, faced a problem, and so did judicious theatre-goers who were not content simply to let the words work. The problem was reconciling this undoubted English genius, a source of pride, with one's sense of being rather provincial in going on liking him when he wasn't, in particular, French, or like Racine (or like what Racine was thought to be).

One surface reason for the discontinuity therefore appears at the level of the vulgar aesthetic of the period. All periods since the renaissance have had their vulgar aesthetic, and much confusion they have caused : one has always to work through the tough skin of this academic theorizing before coming on what people might actually allow themselves to feel and like, as distinct from what they thought they ought to. The vulgar aesthetic of the so-called enlightenment is summed up as neo-classicism. In terms of cultural nationalism it was a device for advancing French dominance. The French literary art-forms were primarily applied to the drama : they were nominally derived from Italian theorists and academic dramatists; actually they put forward a stereotype which claimed to represent the practice and authority of Corneille and Racine, and especially in matters of external form.

The root doctrine was *vraisemblance*, a word which cannot easily be translated. 'Verisimilitude' is the nearest word we have, but it begs as many questions as the original. It is certainly not a matter of 'realism'—though it has been plausibly argued that theatrical realism is the ultimate result of a concern for *vraisemblance*. (The ultimate and crippling question asked by a stickler for verisimilitude is 'Why are these people speaking in verse?') At the beginning of this historical process what we have is a set of hardened conventions. At the lowest structural level of all there is a concern with giving the characters a plausible reason for coming on and off stage, so that the linking of scenes (in French drama a new scene begins with every entrance or exit) shall seem natural or logical. This is a drama in which people only talk, since if they were to do anything more the duller-witted or more theoretically-minded in the audience might well consider that this simulated action was only a simulated action, and the theatrical illusion might be 'strained'. Given, then, that they only talk, the characters also need good reasons and likely occasions for talking to each other. That concern does produce a well-constructed play, in a narrow sense. Indeed in Racine's hands, where the reasons are always an urgent internal pressure, so that the main characters can't keep away from each other, it produces an almost seamless action. In others, it can be a merely external concern, producing a sequence of tiresomely anxious self-justifications.

The other great concern, a related one, was the doctrine of the unities: of time, place and action. These actually produced some fairly strenuous implausibilities: if everything in the action has to take place on one unvarying spot, you somehow have to get your characters passing and repassing that one spot, and the concern becomes distracting and artificial. The place itself has to be some neutral locality such that all the characters can plausibly come and go, and the effect is of a premature railway-station waiting-room. If everything has to take place within at most twenty-four hours, you may again strain credulity. The requirement gave Racine the incentive to plan a massively impending set of forces in tension, which are released at the beginning of the play and rapidly work themselves out, with dismaying remorselessness. Other neo-classical dramatists merely found themselves with an unmanageable amount going on, in a to-and-fro of movement which could not conceivably be accomplished in a day (Johnson's *Irene* is a case in point, and so is Voltaire's *Zaïre*). The only recourse is a studied vagueness about how long it is all actually taking. It would have been more plausible and less of a strain—more *vraisemblable*—to admit that it was taking days, weeks, months, or when necessary years. But the spectator is assumed

135

simultaneously to be a literalist idiot, a stickler for the rules, *and* someone who can be hoodwinked by an apparent sticking to the rules.

The other damaging tenets were the preoccupation with decorum and poetic justice. Decorum requires that tragedy should concern only elevated personages, and that they speak in an elevated manner suited to their station. There can be no vernacular simplicity. This was an enormous blow to any spontaneity of utterance, but a bigger blow to poetry as such. A central character who cannot use 'low' words cannot speak much of his language : cannot for instance speak like Othello, Macbeth and the other great Shakespearean characters. Associations are combed out, metaphors with them. Othello's jealousy, if it is to be caught as a real psychic event, must be caught as it is actually felt, or imagined to be felt. As Shakespeare reveals it, it has obsessive elements which when they are brought into the light are actually disgusting. There are similar wild obsessive moments in *Lear* and *Hamlet*. There is no point in translating this into a language of art : it is counterproductive, a censoring or suppression rather than an expression.

(A sidelight here on Lawrence's observation that tragedy in the drama is inherently limited in scope because it does not, cannot, represent the whole of life, is abstracted and ennobled. In the novel, he said, you are always aware that there is a WC on the premises. In *Othello* there is a dungeon-privy in the hero's *mind*. Shakespeare's general grasp of the whole of life exceeds Lawrence's. For one thing, Shakespeare understood people whom Lawrence wrote off as inferior—Othello, for instance, is allowed to grip our understanding as Clifford Chatterley is not. For another thing Shakespeare's earthy, bawdy or obscene language is natural and unforced and dramatically appropriate where Lawrence's dirty words in *Lady Chatterley's Lover* are merely an uncomfortable vibration, a thrill, a willed attempt to be spontaneous.)

As for poetic justice, it required that Shakespeare's greatest plays end otherwise than they do. Cordelia's death is an affront, and so presumably is Desdemona's. By the same token, the end of Monteverdi's *Poppaea* would be profoundly shocking to a neo-classical mind : the triumph of self-exploited sexuality in Poppaea and unrestrained tyranny in Nero may be something we observe in life, but we don't expect it in the classical theatre. The underlying doctrine

136

here is that we are only pleasantly instructed if a conventional morality is underpropped.

Yet Racine's moral universe is not ultimately comforting at all—just the opposite. He subverts the certainties of his time, if one listens to what he is really saying. But it was his gift to give his contemporaries something superficially like the art they expected, with implications that only a few would hear. He also elaborated a *style noble*, an art-language, which seems to have filtered out a lot of the vernacular. Yet it is capable of dire simplicities; and he has that vein of subdued metaphor which seems like smouldering cliché but keeps glowing into life. Phèdre has to experience something as destructive of her social self as Othello : she undergoes that quasi-sexual climax on stage at the end of her scene with Hippolyte, and her language has powerful undertones of violence, degradation, sexuality and even perversity. These are largely derived from the exploration of the psychic meanings of the old myth, which is made active by being taken into the language as a network of motif and metaphor. This is active as part of the meaning of the play, and enables Racine, within a neo-classical mode, to keep a real poetry as a dramatic medium.

Yet it was the final effect of neo-classicism that myth itself was subverted. The enlightened mind cannot be comfortable with 'superstition', and sooner or later it was bound to feel that the active, even violent, substance of Greek mythology was an embarrassment. We do not 'believe in' all this as part of our official creed; why then undergo the strain of trying to make sense of what shocks and disgusts us? This was a further embarrassment because the classical world was constantly adduced as the virtual standard of all art. Can we both wholeheartedly admire and be shocked at the barbarity of it all? The solution is to castrate the ancient world in a number of ways : to reduce it in the first place to a mere repertory of motifs and superficial forms, the fund of allusions by which educated men recognize each other. In the second place myth is replaced by allegory : the old tales, suitably reduced in content, may be used as a kind of algebra in which moral maxims of a very general sort may be encapsulated, and dry, even banal, morals conveyed in a pleasantly figurative dress.

In another respect opera, especially the Venetian and French opera of 'machines' was a powerful solvent of these general problems.

If you are following an old tale, and you are approaching the point where your hero, Orpheus, has to be torn in pieces, or your heroine, Iphigenia, sacrificed; and if you think that your courtly audience is likely to say that it didn't leave the dinner table in order to be depressed and is not therefore going to present you with a diamond-studded snuff box full of gold coins, you bring down a god in a very striking cloud (an impressive effect), the hero or heroine is taken on board, and god and passenger then return aloft, preferably singing. It is understood that the mortal becomes a star: very elegant. Another good device, effective theatrically and demanding less in the way of equipment, is to have an oracular voice issuing from behind the altar, and saying that the gods, who can hardly be less magnanimous than the people on stage (on pain of being thought irrational), are now satisfied with the moral gymnastics just performed by the leading character. If this is sung, by a good bass voice, to the statutory accompaniment of trombones, everyone can feel the evening is well spent, and the metaphysical tension is dispelled. When Goethe was in danger of having a tragedy at the end to his *Egmont*, the hero of Netherlands nationalism is vouchsafed a vision of his own future fame—a well-lit tableau, with the allegorical figure of fame awarding the martyr-victim his crown. It is an updated version of the old apotheosis. Egmont leaves, to be executed offstage after the curtain has gone down, but it is the apotheosis that remains in the memory and cheers one up. Schiller summed it up neatly and mordantly as a '*salto mortale* into the operatic'. So much the worse for the operatic, one is in some danger of thinking.

I have shown, I hope, that Racine in *Phèdre* made the myth active. He could do the same for the Old Testament typological myth in *Athalie*. But it has to be noted that in *Iphigènie* he allowed his heroine to escape being sacrificed. Since he had thought at one point that Quinault and Lully were trivializing myth in their music drama, it should be recorded that he had a moment of weakness himself.

In the end even the passions are domesticated by these processes and this art. Since we are human we know in a general way that we are subject to them; but a truly edifying drama will show us rising above them—unlike Othello, unlike Phèdre. The soul of the noble person is a theatre in which there may be witnessed a conflict between merely private passions, usually love or jealousy, and the feeling of social obligation, usually the duty of an enlightened ruler

138

to show magnanimity. The conflict takes place : the noble soul is shown in tension. The conflict is resolved when the high-born person asserts his social or caste self : the passion, knowing itself vanquished, and acquiescing in the victory, disappears like something purged away.

This too is the stuff of opera, and specifically of *opera seria*. The first 'reform' of the opera was that carried out by Apostolo Zeno. Of this Schlegel drily observes

> Even before Metastasio, Apostolo Zeno had, as it is called, purified the opera, a phrase which in the sense of modern critics often means emptying a thing of its substance and vigour.

It would not now be possible for a Monteverdi to have a comic nurse in a serious opera, nor for vice to be so splendidly triumphant. Schlegel goes on :

> He formed it on the model of tragedy, and more especially of French tragedy; and a too faithful or rather too slavish approximation to this model is the very cause why he left so little room for musical development, on which account his pieces were immediately driven from the stage of the opera by his more expert successor.

This was of course Metastasio, who with Alfieri declared

> that in order to preserve their own originality, they purposely avoided reading the French models. But this very precaution appears somewhat suspicious : whoever feels himself perfectly firm and secure in his own independence, may without hesitation study the works of his predecessors; he will thus be able to derive from them many an improvement in his art, and yet stamp on his own productions a peculiar character. But there is nothing on this head that I can urge in support of these poets : if it be really true that they never, or not before the completion of their works, perused the works of French tragedians, some invisible influence must have diffused itself through the atmosphere which, without their being conscious of it, determined them.

This is not a mere sarcasm; as Schlegel very well knew. He goes on :

> This is at once conceivable from the great estimation which, since the time of Louis XIV, French Tragedy had enjoyed, not only with the learned, but also with the great world throughout Europe; from the new modelling of several foreign theatres to the fashion

of the French; from the prevailing spirit of criticism, in which negative correctness was everything, and in which France gave the tone to the literature of other countries. The affinity is in both undeniable, but from the intermixture of the musical element in Metastasio, it is less striking than in Alfieri.

It would be a simple exercise to take Metastasio's libretti or those of his imitators, and demonstrate the Racinian properties. Yet they are only properties in the stage-sense, and they are at the service of an implicit dialectic which is Cornelian. The aria of torment or indecision in the central character is descended from Rodrigue's *stances* in *Le Cid*, and is resolved in the Cornelian manner: the hero preserves his integrity. It can only be minor characters (Elettra in *Idomeneo*, for instance) who find that their jealousy *won't* go away, who express this in a fierce exit aria and rush off to ... what? Suicide perhaps; anyway that sort of irredeemable passion has to be got off the stage before the comforting finale. And audiences listening to the 'romantic' Violetta in Verdi's *La Traviata* may fleetingly wonder why in the succession of expressive rhythms she passes through in Act II, Scene 1 she breaks into the march-rhythm of '*Morró! morró!*' and is joined in that rhythm by the elder Germont, who catches her exaltation. It would be too simple to say that Verdi just liked march-rhythms. They express proud resolve, that victory of the noble soul over its own desires or weaknesses inaugurated by Corneille and taken by Metastasio into *opera seria*. Nor is this merely naïve. A genuine nobility seeking expression in a courtly art will want its highest values expressed in that art. The highest value, if it was not to be 'I have power over others' must be 'I have power over myself'. As Corneille's Auguste put it in *Cinna*:

> Je suis maître de moi comme de l'univers :
> Je le suis; je veux l'être.

> *I am master of myself as I am of the universe:*
> *I am so; I will myself to be so.*

One respects this as an ideal, and as the source of a great deal of valuable art; it nonetheless strikes us as less real than the insight of Racine. He pays tribute to the social ideal, since failure to fulfil it requires the death of his chief characters. We assent to the death of Phèdre, and so to the values she judges herself by, or we seem to.

140

But if we really feel her passion (and her language is such that we can feel it) we know how hopeless her situation is, and how far she is from any imagined world in which noble natures simply dominate their impulses. In her the passions are not domesticated : the image in which love is apprehended and explored is the predatory wild beast fixed on the back of a dying victim.

9

Towards Romanticism

What happened in Spain in the eighteenth century is in its own way representative of European movements of taste. Calderón died in 1681, in a kind of apotheosis. There was no thought then that he was not a supremely great European dramatist. The time of his maturity was the period of Spanish political hegemony; and it was not apparent to him or to anyone else that as the continental political situation changed the Spanish would lose self-confidence, and confidence also in their own culture.

In his own lifetime, he did fall foul of neo-classical armchair critics ('bookish theorics', to use Iago's good phrase); he lost some favour after the death of Felipe IV in 1665. But he went on writing *autos*, the peculiarly Spanish form : and he went on being acted— long after his death he retained that essential popularity in the theatre, where people may not know anything about art, but know what they like. That is not merely a Philistine posture : it can be the saving of art, just because it is honest.

But in 1700 Carlos II of Spain died, having made his heir Philippe d'Anjou, the Bourbon pretender and grandson of Louis XIV. Hence the war of the Spanish Succession, and the Treaty of Utrecht, which confirmed Philippe as, indeed, Felipe V. The consequences for Spanish culture were very great. There followed all the good and bad effects of *afrancesamiento* : the formation of a Royal Academy, where writers become approved, even immortal, in their own lifetime by official act of incorporation; where taste becomes codified and institutional, where the language gets, as it were, dry cleaned and pressed and is paraded in an official dictionary with all its proper meanings displayed and the others either ignored or certified as vulgar or obscene—where in short the arts get severed from any popular origins; which are forgotten or ignored in the way that ignoble parvenus are ashamed of the relatives they left behind them in the provinces.

142

The relatives were the great geniuses of the Spanish stage, insofar as their art could not be made to look anything but popular and national. The canons of neo-classicism were duly set out for Spanish audiences in critical treatises, for instance the *Poética* of Luzán. The depressing aspect of these works in Spain is that the French line was taken whole. Addison or Johnson in England, basically honest men of individual judgement, were not able and did not wish to persuade themselves that Shakespeare, Milton, even the old English ballads, were not things to enjoy and admire; so a case had to be made for them, an appeal allowed (as they put it) from art to nature. One had to make reservations, to the effect that Shakespeare's age was 'rude', the language untamed, the rules of art unfortunately unknown; but, that said, one could insist that human nature was fundamentally one beneath surfaces of politeness, and that Shakespeare was a great English genius. Nothing can please many and please long, Johnson said, but just representations of general nature. Shakespeare had evidently pleased many and pleased long; he *must* therefore offer that representation. Shakespeare opened to the reader or playgoer a school of humanity, or encyclopaedia of the passions; and studying his work you learnt something true and useful about human nature.

Luzán saw that the *auto* was uniquely Spanish; that it was an allegorical representation in honour of the eucharist; that because of its peculiar nature it was free of any rules; and he praised Calderón as writer of *autos*. But turning to popular Spanish drama as a whole, he felt bound to condemn it as 'licentious' in its freedom and tending therefore to the corruption of art. Its lack of 'verisimilitude'; its free use of myth; all the things one might call 'musical'—the oracular voices, the stichomythia, the echo-scenes, the use of song itself—all these popular elements made Spanish drama something which was wildly beyond the 'rules of art' : hence a 'corruption which took deeper hold day by day, to the point where the nation lost all good taste, and literature went down to its total decadence'. These were the words of Luis Jose Velázquez, whose *Origins of Castilian Poetry* (1754), the first history of Spanish poetry, faithfully followed Luzán's general line about the popular drama.

The attack was pressed. Carlos III came to the throne in 1759, and there followed a period of extreme subordination to French cultural imperialism. The *autos* were banned in 1765, having been attacked in Clavijo's *Pensador,* a journal founded in 1762 on the model of the English *Spectator.* The ninth issue attacked the *autos,* fundamentally because, being popular, simple and allegorical, they seemed to Clavijo barbaric and proletarian, crude and mixed in mode.

But the banning of the *autos* had a significance beyond this uneasy contempt for a merely popular form. It was a fundamental tenet of neo-classicism that art and religion had to be kept apart. Johnson, writing as a deeply religious man, explained that if art was primarily a matter of 'imitation' or 'simulation'—therefore at a remove from real experience—the true believer was bound to be shocked at seeing his deepest beliefs and feelings merely simulated. The direct expression of religious feeling was found in the ceremonies of the church, or in one's private devotions. This was a deep matter between the individual and God; or between the congregation of believers and God. Art had nothing to offer which the believer did not feel as direct intuition or as matter of dogmatic belief, and it was a profanation publicly and in a lay context to represent or display or simulate or paraphrase these things.

From an entirely different point of view, Voltaire made very similar remarks. Whatever he was, Voltaire was not a Christian. In his *Dictionnaire Philosophique,* under the heading *'Art dramatique',* he mocked at the *auto.* For Voltaire it was a sense of decorum rather than a firm belief which automatically separated religion from a secular art like drama. From these two different standpoints drama was devalued, and cut off from its deepest and oldest roots. The *auto* was the last survivor in Europe of the gravest strand of popular drama : the festival drama in which the people represent their deepest faith (last, that is, unless Wagner is taken to have revived that tradition).

Voltaire is of course important in the whole European story, since he was for a time almost an arbiter of European culture : he represented the dominant French tradition, and he was enterprising enough to survey, though not fundamentally serious enough to comprehend, the other traditions which might be considered as competitors or alternatives. He took some interest both in Spanish and in English drama, and plagiarized both, in a superficial way, in his own plays.

Calderón's *En esta vida, toda es verdad y toda mentira* has the same plot and characters as Corneille's *Héraclius.* Which was the earlier play and which influenced the other? It seemed to matter because Voltaire found himself arguing that Calderón, the barbarian, must have been first, so that his dross could be removed in the refining process carried out by Corneille. There was a controversy from 1724 onwards; and in 1762 Voltaire produced a paraphrastic summary of the Spanish play, rather in the mode of Tolstoy's unfortunate comments on *Lear*. Voltaire made the pronouncement that

> In short, it matters little to the progress of the arts to know who was the first author of a dozen lines of verse. What matters is to know what is good or bad, what is well or badly constructed, well or badly expressed, and to form just impressions of an art for so long barbarous, now prosecuted in the whole of Europe, and almost perfected in France.

That puts the neo-classical position neatly. He went on :

> It is natural that Corneille should have found a little gold in Calderón's dunghill.

He was to apply the same figure to Shakespeare. He had visited England in 1726, to learn what might be learnt by a Frenchman. He admired English constitutional arrangements and political thought : he valued the tradition of empiricism and English achievements in science. He went to the theatre, and observed that Shakespeare was acted and read. He thought rather well of *Julius Caesar* in particular. This was reported to the consciously superior French in 1733 in the *Lettres philosophiques*. Voltaire went on to borrow discreetly : from *Othello* in his *Zäire*; from *Hamlet* in *Eriphyle*, and from *Macbeth* in *Mahomet*.

It was one thing to admit from a general position of condescension, that the archaic writer Shakespeare, still admired parochially in his own country, had elements of genius. This could be said by someone absolutely confident that Racine was better, and that the French classical theatre represented virtual perfection. As the century wore on (and Voltaire with it) he began to repent what seemed to him to have been his excessive generosity, since it had induced people of uncertain or bad taste to admire more of Shakespeare than was decent. Voltaire felt he had been a Frankenstein, fathering this monster, and in 1776 he poured scorn on the taste he had fostered, and found Shakespeare too to be a dunghill, in which there were scattered jewels.

145

One might take this change, between 1733 and 1776, as evidence of a turn in the tide of taste. In the first quarter of the eighteenth century neo-classical orthodoxy was scarcely questioned; in the last quarter of the century it was under serious attack, could even be considered defeated. What was at stake here was a whole set of related issues : the idea of an academic tragedy which pleased because it followed the rules and therefore satisfied taste; the assumption that Racine in particular 'pleased' for that reason; French cultural dominance; the estimation of other national traditions and in particular their great exemplars, Shakespeare and Calderón. By the end of the century, Racine, because he was identified with mere neo-classicism, was considered to have been worsted in this strange literary battle. Shakespeare (throughout Europe) and Calderón (in Germany and to some extent in his native Spain) had become the hero-figures of an awaited romantic drama which was to be everything neo-classicism was not. The idea of nationalism in the drama was revived, but it became a nationalism of conscious folklore and historical reconstruction. The rules were loosened, if not jettisoned, and drama became freer. For a time it was rather assumed that this new drama must be in verse. But the drama produced by European romanticism was not at all a poetic drama in the old sense; and this in the end must tell us something about the language used, and the degree of inwardness with the characters that it produced or permitted.

The agencies which secured first the survival and then the triumph of Shakespeare and Calderón were of three kinds : the actors, the translators, and the scholars and critics. The actors kept the old dramatists on the stage and in peoples' hearts and minds; the translators gave them a European audience beyond their own country; the scholars produced editions and commentaries which secured their text as classic authors, while the critics gave them a new and greater significance. One should add a fourth, later, group, where the process begins to effect transformations in art as a whole; the later writers and especially the composers for whom Shakespeare became a living influence affecting their own work.

The actors should be placed first, because it was they who first took Shakespeare and Calderón into Europe. In the theatres of what was in the late seventeenth century the Spanish Netherlands, wandering troupes of actors performed Calderón and Shakespeare— simplified and adapted, but still offered as the great named dramatists the recent past. There were no serious linguistic barriers between the Low Countries and North Germany, so that audiences in Hamburg heard Calderón—heard him transformed also into early opera. The first process—acting—quickly passed into the second, translation : versions (or rather reductions) of both authors were provided for acting purposes. These should be distinguished from the 'literary' translations which came later and were meant to provide a discriminating public readers with versions which were less reductive, and meant to be pondered and not just heard in the playhouse. When literary translations were available, then their being acted in an important dramatic centre became another kind of event, much more important than an occasional performance by a strolling troupe. That event could in turn be signalled by an important critic : for instance Lessing, the resident dramaturgist at Hamburg, who during his brief period of office organized the repertoire, provided some of the plays, and by writing important criticism after the event turned a mere season at a Hamburg theatre into something of historical importance beyond the boundaries of Germany.

Lessing started from the position that Germany, unlike Spain, England and France, had no national dramatic tradition, and needed one. If Germans looked across their borders their eyes fell first on France : culturally self-confident, even colonialist, making the sort of claim for French classical tragedy that Voltaire was making. In their modesty, Germans like the pliable and mediocre Gottsched would accept the French model as the European model, but Lessing though they were wrong. He was among the first to advance the anticlassical, anti-French 'hard line' :

> those who boast of having had a theatre for a hundred years, aye, who boast of having the best theatre in all Europe—even the French have as yet no theatre, certainly no tragic one. The impressions produced by French tragedy are so shallow, so cold . . .

Lessing took Voltaire at his word, and examined his plays in detail, and also the theories of the neo-classic doctrinaires taken as truly representative of the French achievement. Pulling the rug from underneath that confident posturing was not really so difficult, though it was an achievement, and a necessary one. It was Racine who suffered, and went on suffering in estimation for ever after.

What would Lessing offer as alternative model? The poet Shakespeare : 'Shakespeare and Shakespeare only and alone'. It was the beginning of what might be called in Goethe's phrase the *Shakespeare ohne Ende* movement. 'But is it always Shakespeare, always and eternally Shakespeare who understood everything better than the French, I hear my readers ask? That exasperates us, since we cannot read him. I seize this opportunity to remind the public of what it seems of purpose to have forgotten. We have a translation of Shakespeare.'

Translations of Shakespeare in the mid- to late eighteenth century look strange to a reader today, largely because they were so careful not to render the original with the literalness or accuracy which would have totally dismayed a reader brought up in the neo-classical taste. Shakespeare was freely adapted, or 'civilized'. The French translation by Ducis, the German prose translation by Wieland, fall far short of a complete rendering. They were a start, however. One may assume also that the support given by the great actors, Talma in France or Friedrich Ludewig Schröder in Hamburg, trod the same kind of tightrope : that audiences saw something which blended the reassuringly familiar classical style of their favourite performer with something which claimed to be free, romantic, or even a little wild—but which would strike us today as conventional theatricality of a very traditional kind. No doubt something similar was going on in England itself : the Shakespearean performances of Garrick, Mrs Siddons and Kemble were appreciated as just or well-considered by a classically minded generation. It was in the 1820s that the torrential passion of Kean (which degenerated by all accounts into a rather unintelligent kind of barnstorming) seized 'romantically' minded audiences as fundamentally more 'true'; and this spectacle was exported to Paris, where the fine flower of the romantic generation— writers, artists and composers—was bowled over. By then Shakespeare had won.

Racine had 'lost' by not being properly represented in the argument. We can be sure that intelligent and sensitive readers in France knew how to appreciate him, and he went on being performed by the official theatre (not entirely an advantage). We know, for instance, that Berlioz responded deeply to him, because we can find traces of *Athalie* in *L'enfance du Christ*, and Berlioz' own libretti tended naturally to be written in a somewhat loose alexandrine, which naturally affects the syllabic underlay of the music. But Stendhal, for instance, in *Racine et Shakespeare*, made no attempt to characterize the great national dramatist correctly—but then he made Shakespeare into a peculiar romantic property as well.

If Shakespeare had 'won' and Racine 'lost', Calderón assumed an equivocal position as a kind of naturalized ancestor of the German theatre. Johann Andreas Dieze became professor of Literary History at Göttingen in 1773; he took a special interest in Spain and Portugal, translated Velázquez' *History* and added abundant notes. He deprecated the tendency of the Spaniards to undervalue their own classics precisely because they were national and popular. He assembled the finest German library of Iberian literature and criticism at Göttingen; and there Tieck and the Schlegels were able to study Spanish literature, with important consequences.

Tieck, the translator of Shakespeare, also wrote plays of his own on Spanish models. He saw Calderón as what he was : the last great poet of Catholicism, a mystic, the guardian and continuator of a tradition going back to the Middle Ages, the leading dramatist of a popular national theatre. In 1798 he read the greatest *auto*, the *Devoción de la Cruz*, and made A. W. Schlegel read it too. He wrote an essay in epistolary form on the Spanish theatre in 1803, and produced two volumes of plays translated from the Spanish in 1804. These translations reproduced the intricate Spanish verse-forms exactly, and in their overall faithfulness matched the extraordinary enterprise of the Schlegel-Tieck translation of Shakespeare, which impresses as both a very faithful translation and a work of literature.

Both Calderón and Shakespeare were in part being used, as distinct from being valued in themselves. The campaign to establish a German literary consciousness, a German national tradition in poetry and the drama, required as forerunners sanctified figures who were not French, and called for a summary view of literary history which might be summed up in these terms : France fell into the error of deeming its tragedy part of a classical continuum which did not really exist. As a result of that error she separated herself from the medieval Christian and romantic tradition (that is to say the tradition of romance, which really existed, hypostatized into a 'romantic' tradition which could supply the Germans with a different false continuum). This had produced a willed and unspontaneous imitation, in France, of the Greco-Latin system. England and Spain,

149

however, remaining faithful to their 'romantic' character, both survived French classicism, at the cost of some ephemeral and superficial classicizing. Calderón represents the vein of indigenous romanticism in the Spanish Peninsula. So universal is the romantic spirit (and one remembers that the classical spirit was thought universal too) that Germany could be seen as forming a unity with romantic England and Spain, and could seek inspiration in medieval history just as Shakespeare and Calderón had done.

This turns the French doctrine neatly on its head. The notion of a continuum is false in both cases. The Germans were declaring a counter-allegiance to the one claimed by France, and in doing so they were declaring that they proposed to impose a new meaning on literary history. The practical advantage was that Shakespeare and Calderón became highly valued, in rather general terms. It is another matter to see authors as they are, and to become inward with that.

The critic Solger, for instance, pointed to the fixed concepts of love, honour, religion and chivalry in Calderón. These were socially and historically determined : interesting insights into the Spain of the time, but not timelessly available. They lead to formulaic use : to conventionality, perfunctoriness, lack of depth. Drama needs and springs from a mythology of some sort. It was both the advantage and disadvantage of Spanish drama that the social thought and feeling of the time was so 'given'—or that the drama accepted it as such and dramatized it as a debate which never went behind given terms. As one result Spanish drama did not produce a Shakespearean exploration of human complexity. If someone in Shakespeare formulates a belief, this is not an abstract statement or debating gambit; it is inseparable from the person speaking and his reasons for wanting to believe it, or what his belief tells us about him. Spanish drama is in that respect humanly less rich. Its highest point, the *auto*, is at best a symbolic representation, at worst an allegory. Which was it? It was important to say, since the distinction between symbol and allegory is central to romantic critical thought.

Certain master-ideas of the German romantic critics had great influence and lasting importance—remain, indeed, the foundation of modern aesthetics, criticism and scholarship.

It had been the basic principle of neo-classicism as of rationalism that the human reason is pure, identical and unchanging. What pleases reason must always please it. If therefore a form of art is elaborated which is founded on rationality and pleasing to reasonable social beings, art has ipso facto been perfected, and the model so produced cannot reasonably be departed from. It was a universalist trap; and the obverse of the doctrine was that the art of rude and irrational ages could not please now, since we have left behind the infancy of the arts, and entered on an unchanging maturity.

Romantic criticism took the opposite line. Art springs from and is of its time and its people. A national art begins by being popular, and it was now a prime need to recover the native spontaneity, imaginative strength, and figurative expressiveness of a popular art (not, actually, a thing you can will). A more developed art, attentive not to external rules but to the needs of its own expressive unfolding, is characterized by organic form—the concept touched on in Coleridge's formulation at the beginning of the previous chapter. Coleridge's predecessors and mentors were the German critics. It was Lessing who was first to point out, in the context of dramatic criticism, that works of art are not composed by being put together to a conventional plan from prefabricated components : the full realization of a complex dramatic conception produces

> another world, a world whose chance events may be connected in a different order, but must still be connected logically . . . a world of genius which transposes, reduces, heightens the particles of the present world in order to form a whole therefrom . . .

and this 'whole' is, in present-day jargon, a 'system'—

> rounded in itself and complete, fully explained in itself, where no difficulty arises to which a solution is not found in [the author's] plan. We ought not to be forced to seek a reason outside, in the general plan of things.

It was Lessing also who pointed out that the vehicle or medium of Shakespeare's art was the language itself : he saw in the primitive London theatre with its open stage and few bare properties not a poverty but a richness, a total freedom; he quoted Cibber's remark that there was nothing to help the spectator's understanding or to assist the actor's performance but 'bare imagination'—nothing, that is, but the verse, and the performance for which it is the score.

Related to the rediscovery of popular participation in the representation of something pertaining to the national consciousness or the 'community of feeling' was the rediscovery of the need for myth, which is the deeper level of all such communication and performance. Myth was now seen not as embarrassing superstition but as a basic form of figurative expression, and this led to a new sense of the relationship between 'primitive' religion and its poetry and mythology. Poetry, said Herder, is a natural kind of prophesying. It became clear that the Bible was, among other things, the mythology and heroic poetry of a pastoral people—like Homer, that is. It became clear that poetic myth is the stuff of natural religion, and that a science of hermeneutics or interpretation would take as its province all religion and all literature. In both it would take its point of departure in the consideration of *form*. The classical Greek dramatists, Shakespeare, the Spanish dramatists, came into a new focus: not as primitives for whom a classically-minded reader could find extenuations, but as the summits of previous literatures that criticism must value, and which a modern drama (perhaps a modern opera too) should emulate.

The German scholar with whom Coleridge had most contact was the philosopher Schelling, with whom he shared a theological interest in hermeneutics—leading to a view of the spiritual unity of the Bible as the document of an evolving communal religious experience. The two men also pondered the distinction between myth and allegory. Schelling had produced the formulation that a people is a *Gemeinschaft des Bewusstseins*—a community of consciousness; that poetry is the expressive product of myth, not an allegorical form which uses myth as an algebra of direct parallelisms or easy equivalences which 'explain' but trivialize it; that religion is itself an evolving element of racial consciousness in which the 'primitive' or mythological stage is not to be discarded *as* 'primitive'; that myth tends to emphasize its own form, whereas in allegory form is only a veil, where the 'meaning' is the real substance; that 'symbol' is itself a difficult term leading to confusions or dissociations of image and sense. Indeed Schelling adopted Coleridge's term 'tautegory' as an opposite of 'allegory': the myth contains within itself a significance which cannot be otherwise expressed, and is multivalent. The only access to it is performance, ritual, reenactment; to try to express these things as 'meaning' or 'doctrine' is to substitute reductive paraphrase, to try to say in different words what you ought to express in the

152

performance itself. The link with Mendelssohn's thought about music becomes clear. The implications for the criticism of poetic drama are also clear. So is the ultimate significance for Wagner's music drama, which aims to revitalize myth in the service of a festival drama which appeals to a recovered community of consciousness.

In immediate practical effect, the most influential of these critics was A. W. Schlegel. His translations of Shakespeare and Calderón have been mentioned. He was a genuinely international influence. His comparison of the *Hippolytus* of Euripides and Racine's *Phèdre* —the *Comparaison des deux Phèdres*—was written in French and published in Paris in 1807. It is a wilful disparagement of Racine, and helped to cement the stereotyped view of him. His famous *Lectures* on the history of drama were given in Vienna in 1808, and were rapidly translated into French and English. They make a very substantial volume, reviewing the whole history of European drama from the Greeks to Goethe and Schiller. The French achievement and the related classical Italian drama is once more disparaged (Racine being given very little attention), and the romantic theatre of England and Spain exalted. Shakespeare is given exhaustive treatment. In short, literary history was drastically rewritten by a master who had actually read in the original all, or nearly all, that he wrote about, and approached it from a genuinely historical standpoint, though one has to grant a *parti-pris* against Racine. The demolition of Voltaire is, I believe, unbiased :

> by turns philosopher, rhetorician, sophist and buffoon . . . [he] made use of poetry as a means to accomplish ends foreign and extrinsecal to it; and this has often polluted the artistic purity of his compositions. Thus, the end of his *Mahomet* was to portray the dangers of fanaticism, or rather, laying aside all circumlocution, of a belief in revelation . . . Universally known as he was to be a bitter enemy of Christianity, he bethought himself of a new triumph for his vanity; in *Zaïre* and *Alzire* he had recourse to Christian sentiments to excite emotion; and here, for once, his versatile heart, which indeed in its momentary ebullitions was not unsusceptible of good feelings, shamed the rooted malice of his understanding; he actually succeeded . . .

The positive effect of these lectures was inestimable, since they are a kind of textbook which is still full of insight, and unrivalled in width of understanding as well as depth. Once again the central

153

tenets of romantic criticism are deployed : especially the formal and expressive function of poetry and the notion of organic form :

> in the fine arts all genuine forms are organic, i.e. determined by the content of the work of art. In a word, form is nothing but a significant exterior, the speaking physiognomy of everything.

But this reinstatement of the notion of poetic drama, and this recovery of Shakespeare, Calderón and Lope was one thing. The best literary consciousness of the early nineteenth century was made aware of the awe-inspiring greatness of Shakespeare and the general desirability of a revived poetic drama. The actual social conditions which might produce such a drama and an audience for it did not exist. The 'community of consciousness' was no longer one, but fractured : for instance, by loss of faith, and by evolving class-consciousness. Tastes had diverged, so that it was no longer possible for the educated unselfconsciously to enjoy what was popular. The popular, not being in touch with the best intelligence, degenerated. The theatre had actually been harmed by the neo-classicizing bent, since it produced a false 'good taste' associated with learning, class, or cosmopolitanism : honest people lost faith in it and lost touch with it. There had been no novel in the renaissance period to compete with drama as the favoured medium of general literary consciousness. Finally, poetry in the nineteenth century consciously withdrew itself from the drama as from other public spheres. At its best, it was the organ of a solitary and silent self-consciousness that required to be meditated, not heard. So the drama was no longer in touch with the highest reaches of the language.

10

The Nineteenth Century:
Drama, Poetry and Music

It is time we had a revival of interest in romantic drama. I use the word 'romantic' to include some authors the Germans themselves think of as classical. From the standpoint of European literary history, Schiller and Goethe, Kleist, Grillparzer and Hebbel all need to be seen in relationship with Lamartine, Musset, Dumas and Hugo. We should add, for the sake of completeness, Wordsworth, Coleridge, Keats, Shelley and Byron; though readers of English do not think of them as dramatists, they all felt that they had as a matter of self-respect to attempt a verse-drama. This is partly because they were countrymen of Shakespeare, partly because they were contemporaries of Kemble and Kean, partly because they were aware of Goethe and Schiller, and the genuine growth of a national school of drama in Germany.

It is foolish to attempt to characterize all the plays of this very fertile period which also included, let us not forget, a good deal of very bad popular romantic drama from the pen or in the style of Kotzebue, the great German exponent of the jerked tear and the throbbing heart. It is generally agreed that Schiller was a very fine dramatist, and so in a related way was Victor Hugo. Neither of them, however, wrote a poetic drama of the kind practised by Shakespeare and Racine. They wrote plays in verse, but the verse is a rhetorical vehicle, not a poetic one. Goethe was a poet (I imply that Schiller was not) but as a man of the theatre his contribution is equivocal. The plays of his which are actable are not in my special-ized sense poetic dramas. *Faust* is not in practical terms a theatre-play at all; and as a work of literature it does not have organic form, as Friedrich Schlegel was the first to say. It is essentially something to read, and to meditate : an entirely idiosyncratic and original work which needs to be taken simply as itself. It inaugurates unmistakably that tendency among romantic writers with dramatic ambitions to produce dramas which cannot be staged and are not meant to be. Hugo's *Cromwell* is another such monster : a historical drama set in England, and amazingly observing the unity of time, since it chronicles the events of a single crucial day. It would also take at least twelve hours to stage, thus carrying *vraisemblance* to a new length. It has Walter Scott's concern for historical truth and local colour, so from that point of view it is like a novel laid out as a drama. But really *Cromwell* and *Faust* are most of all like a form of mental television, a scenario for a film, for projection in the mind of the solitary reader in his armchair. The imagination, it is implied, is the ideal theatre.

So it is; but we are on the way to a kind of literary solipsism. It was supported by a general disgust with the theatre as such in the 'sensitive' who, then as now, pointed out that any actual production of Shakespeare (for instance) is in the hands of possibly indifferent and probably stupid actors, who don't fully understand the detail of the verbal texture, mangle the rhythms of the verse, are normally exhibitionist by definition, brought up in bad acting traditions, and directed by some egoist with a fashionable bright idea about the 'meaning' of the play which he imposes whether it is good or bad. All that was, is, and will be true. One thing that it calls for is good dramatic criticism which reasserts the common sense of readers and audiences who genuinely possess the central meanings of their classics. But on arguments like this, romantic poets after their quasi-obligatory attempts at a stage-piece more and more withdraw from the public theatre, attempting at most a closet-drama or armchair drama or drama for a never-attained 'ideal' theatre.

The successes and failures of romantic drama can be ascribed to common debts : the domination of Shakespeare was exercised through a narrow range of his plays; and this gave the romantic poet-dramatists a conventional and surprisingly shallow notion of what a poetic drama was—what constituted freedom from the constricting mould of French neoclassicism.

Friedrich Schlegel gives a clue to this process. He was interested in a national drama as expressive of the national consciousness; it was natural to turn to Shakespeare's histories as models. *Henry V*, he asserted, represents the summit of Shakespeare's power. Schiller's

156

'passionate rhetoric', Schlegel knew, was not poetry, but it was effective drama of this kind, and Schiller's political energy, in *Don Carlos* for instance, was inevitably found sympathetic by nascent liberalism. The same note, characteristically shortcircuited by Goethe's ultimate insouciance, is heard in *Egmont*. The political concern which makes Schiller an activist could in other dramatists be turned into something merely theatrical—spectacular, histrionic, 'epic' in the Hollywood sense. (This was supported by the increasing size of contemporary stages, and the development of scenic design and costume detail. The specific romantic three—carried into Grand Opera—is the long-drawn-out procession in a grandiose setting with a cast of many supers—or a chorus—in authentic costume.) Shakespeare's histories foster this taste, and gave Grillparzer, for instance, some of his characters (his Ottokar is a mixture of Macbeth and Richard III; his Rudolf is Henry V), gave him also his form, his iambic, and even literal verbal echoes. But knowledge of *Macbeth* taught Grillparzer nothing about tragedy as something to do with the depth of individuality. It took Victor Hugo's genuinely epic imagination to turn the romantic heroic pageant into something original and stirring—in *Hernani*, for instance, where in his colossal soliloquy before the tomb of Charlemagne Don Carlos turns before our eyes into the 'world-historical man' Charles V, having begun the play as a standard romantic anti-hero. *Hernani* shows another Shakespearean influence : that of *Romeo and Juliet*, which had had since Lessing's advocacy a peculiar power—leading in due course to *Tristan*.

The Histories and *Romeo and Juliet* : they make two kinds of fatality accessible, neither of them necessarily or intrinsically tragic. The first is the fatality of historical process—the working-out of vast political and dynastic processes on a European stage. The two really great achievements in this line are Schiller's *Wallenstein* and Hugo's epic moments (in *Hernani*, in *Cromwell*, for instance). This was a real feeling, an excitement; and in the era of Napoleon that active self-realizing energy was a natural interest. But it is the self inflicting itself on the world in action. The corresponding tragic irony—the insignificance of mere action, or the blind reversal of fortune—is equally simple and external. The second fatality is that of young love frustrated by those same impersonal social forces—politics, religion, dynastic interest. This is more tender, more lyrical; but only a self-aware passion has tragic possibilities. Romantic drama has an enormous sense of the theatrical : the *coups de théâtre* in Schiller and Hugo are still electric, the 'strong curtains' still impress. What was lacking was inwardness, a lack inevitably associated with the absence of poetry—all this verse was at best rhetoric or epic inflation. All the ends are external; so is the convention of 'character'. Inevitably therefore this drama is not in the same way as Shakespeare's and Racine's a mirror of the will, in the deepest sense.

The general history of romantic drama might be summed up in this way : with the defeat of neo-classicism and the reinstatement of Shakespeare and Calderón, the founders of a new drama felt it obligatory to make it a poetic one, to challenge the giants of the renaissance, or more modestly to follow them. The attempt was made; where the plays so produced were successful, it was because they managed something that was *not* Shakespearean. Where it was too closely Shakespearean, it was a disaster, especially in England, where good poets who had their own language fell into the trap of writing 'Elizabethan' blank verse, and so produced a more or less distinguished pastiche. Shelley's *The Cenci*, for instance, seemed like a great play to Artaud—who had not enough English to know that it was a pot-pourri of Shakespearean phrases, mostly from *Othello*, and radically incoherent like the product of a ventriloquizing literary ghost. Keats's *Otho the Great*, wisely laid aside unfinished, was meant as a vehicle for Kean, and offered mock-Tudor rhodomontade. Wordsworth was influenced by Schiller in *The Borderers*, which therefore has some of the kinds of cheap thrill made popular by *Die Räuber*; but the other influence is that of Shakespeare. This is, for once, at the deep level : Wordsworth's villain is modelled on Iago, and shows that Wordsworth understood Iago as Coleridge did not. The play is worth reading, but not worth acting. The only English romantic poet who wrote a passable play was Byron. His preposterous *Manfred* was an attempt at an English *Faust* : but his *Marino Faliero* is more like Schiller, reads well, and might act well.

Wordsworth and Byron are closer to success as dramatists for two reasons. First, although Shakespearean reminiscences are lodged in their writing like currants in dough, neither of them affects the Shakespearean dialect as such : they do try to write their own language. Second, their best dramas attempt to seize and project the mind into a human situation, imagined and developed as the interaction of characters who have some depth of motive. Indeed *The*

Borderers is a profound drama if not a good play : for one thing it provides a considered answer to Schiller by taking the basic situation of *Die Räuber* (the romantic anti-hero as leader of a band of social outcasts), overturns its shallow rationalizations, and makes it impossible to succumb to the thrill by showing how a character might be seduced into that pose, and what a burden of guilt he must bear if he becomes conscious of the process. It is the villain, the Iago-figure Oswald, who gives a warning of what he is going to inflict on the hero Marmaduke :

> Action is transitory—a step, a blow,
> The motion of a muscle—this way or that—
> 'Tis done, and in the after-vacancy
> We wonder at ourselves like men betrayed :
> Suffering is permanent, obscure and dark,
> And shares the nature of infinity.

Wordsworth's moral depth is that of the meditative rather than the dramatic imagination. No important drama can be without his insight, but has to combine with it a dramatic gift which can in the end only show itself as a specific feeling for words issuing from the mouth of an imagined person who is not just a split-off element of the author, but becomes part of a self-subsistent world. Musset's *Lorenzaccio*, for instance, combines the local colour and bustle, the hectic activity, of Renaissance Italy (as in Byron's *Marino Faliero*) with a moral insight like Wordsworth's, and produces a great play built round a deeply-conceived central character. It solves the problem of language (how not to be merely Shakespearean, how to escape the echoes of great French predecessors, how not to be, therefore, spurious and stagey) by being in prose. It is not an equivocation to say that Musset's prose is more poetic than Schiller's verse. It combines to an extraordinary degree the racy and the vernacular with the ingenious, the figurative and the exalted. It inaugurates that vein of self-intoxicated French dramatic eloquence which continues into the twentieth century in Giraudoux, Cocteau, Anouilh and Sartre (I imply no comparisons in pointing to a sort of common medium). Musset called his volume *Un spectacle dans un fauteuil*, seeming to renounce the theatre itself, in much the same way as Byron, dedicating *Sardanapalus* to 'the illustrious Goethe', started his preface 'In publishing the following Tragedies I have only to repeat that they were not composed with the most remote view to the stage'. Yet Sarah Bernhardt saw what a tremendous 'vehicle' *Lorenzaccio* offered to an actor of genius, and at the age of 52 played the part for the first time in 1896, in a 'condensed' version. It was a triumph, mostly for her and partly for the play, which has been occasionally revived by the Comédie-Française. It would, like *Faust*, make a fine film; though any film-maker would 'condense' it verbally, as he would *Faust*—that is to say he would plunder its visual drama and sacrifice its verbal drama, therefore its soul and intelligence.

For *Faust*, perhaps for *Wallenstein*, certainly for *Cromwell*, probably for *Danton's Tod*, for *Lorenzaccio*, for *The Borderers*, we are going to have to rely on the theatre of the mind, or at best on radio. If these plays were to be staged, or filmed, or televised, they would be cut or otherwise adapted to meet the demands of the audience— or rather, for fear that an audience would be bored, and would not be willing to meet the demands of the words. The imagination of the romantic poets was not, that is, in the habit of adapting itself to a public or popular medium. There was not now a tradition among poets of assuming that the public forms of the drama, existing as a going concern, and constituting a primary criterion by which one wanted to be judged, had to be mastered; that one had to submit oneself to them as Shakespeare submitted himself. You no longer learnt to please a public and then acquired a right to alter the prescription.

This is a fundamental change. The theatre continues in business because it is able to coax an audience to buy tickets, sit through the performance, and—more often than not—go out pleased, and therefore willing to return. Shakespeare pleased his audience, but gave them more than they bargained for. The theatre is in that sense unalterably a 'popular' art, though the composition of the audience may change very much socially, or rather may change very much in the social tone it chooses to hide behind. Racine's audiences were aristocratic in their tone : it does not follow that they were all nobles —indeed we know they were not. Nineteenth-century theatres tended to divide on social lines : there was an 'art' theatre for the bourgeoisie and a popular theatre for the populace. But the distinction could not be hard and fast : the price of admission was the only real qualification, and one's taste the only real personal impulse to go to one or the other.

The romantic poets tried first to write a drama of which they only knew that it was going to be romantic and poetic. They did not ultimately command either of the potential audiences, still less unite them. They abandoned the theatre to 'commercial' writers, and rationalized the defeat by saying that in any case they despised the theatre. The place and function once occupied by poetic drama was therefore abandoned to opera. This was at first the Grand Opera which was scarcely less vulgar, in obvious external ways, than commercial theatre, but surprisingly often redeemed by the music, which was in its own way popular. There followed the intellectually ambitious music-drama of Wagner, his rivals and followers, which has ever since consistently held the place in intellectual and artistic life which the poetic theatre once held. Only a *wish* to believe that Ibsen did something comparable, together with the theatricality of Ibsen's most successful plays, sustains the belief that Ibsen wrote a poetic drama. Mesmerized by his crude and opportunistic deployment of 'symbols', we ignore their flatness, gratuitousness and thinness, the portentous sketchiness of Ibsen's psychology and the grim aplomb, the solemness, with which the whole affair takes itself. In the moments of embarrassment which nonetheless afflict us, we say it must be better in the original Norwegian. It would need to be : I doubt if it is.

If I am right, Ibsen's admirers (admittedly they outnumber his critics) have taken the will for the deed. It is clear what Ibsen set out to do, and a sign of good nature to agree that he brought it off. Why should so many people have wanted Ibsen to be a success? Because, I think, a success of that kind was certainly needed. The retreat of poets from the theatre, the defeat of romantic drama, meant, I have suggested, that the choice for the theatre-goer was between the remaining vigorous traditions : a prose romanticism which gave theatricality of a spurious sort (Dumas' *Antony*, for instance), the celebrated well-made play of Scribe and its descendants (what in England was thought of until recently as West End Theatre), the popular traditions of pantomime, melodrama, music hall. Alternatively one went to the opera, and in Wagnerian music-drama found the only real nineteenth-century successor to poetic drama. If you felt that opera was drama, you had no problem : *there* was the form in which you found the higher kinds of interest that a poetic drama once offered. If on the other hand you felt, as a poet, or as an upholder of 'legitimate' theatre, that opera was spurious, or exotic, or ridiculous, or merely an enormous and rather threatening inter-loper which had filched dramatic poetry's birthright, you would not be happy until some playwright arrived who reversed the process, and took opera back into words.

Ibsen seemed to have done this. His 'form' is as calculated, as significant, as Wagner's but in dangerously literal ways. What the scenery shows matters : if there is a portrait on the wall you have to know who it represents and what he represents for the drama. If someone, a blonde girl for instance, comes in in a sailor suit, the colour of her hair matters, and the costume is deeply significant. If the sun comes out, it counts; if there is a mountain in sight, that matters too. What people say, though it is horribly stilted, is also remorselessly full of significances, and it is soon plain that they are bandying motives to and fro. These develop little in a poetic sense, but their deeper meaning is either made ludicrously plain or remains savingly obscure.

This last point is concerned with the language, and one has to fall silent when the trump card, knowledge of Norwegian, is produced. But it is a disbelieving silence. In translation, at any rate, there is no sign of the kind of volatility or ductility of Shakespeare's or Racine's metaphors, which have the power to move across logical spaces by setting up extensions of meaning. Ibsen's actual symbols are inert, however much they are commented on. So the wild duck in the play of that name, which gets a great deal of exegesis by the characters, remains an embarrassing property in an otherwise quite interesting and all too comprehensible realistic play. It only serves to blur the edges a bit, so that we can believe we are in the realm of Symbolism. It has been a help, of course, that there is a doctrine that symbols should not be ultimately reduced to explanation, or paraphrased. This has the happy consequence that opportunism, muddle, or mere hopefulness can be redeemed by the blessed word 'ambiguity', much in favour since the 1930s.

The result is that Ibsen's best plays can have the structure of a well-made play on the pattern set by Scribe, where everything func-tions at the level of plausibility, normality, and 'realism'; and where the internal springs of the characters are determined by 'psychology' of a down-to-earth sort. At the other 'level' (and I suppose it was Ibsen who set people talking about works of art functioning at several 'levels of reality') you have the symbolic machinery, which is meant to 'raise' the whole thing to a poetic 'plane'. Soberly considered, it might turn out only to be a device which *seems* to eliminate all gratuitousness from the everyday, and to make it 'significant'; but the significance is only a vagueness. It has to be vague, to avoid being ridiculous or banal. Perhaps it does not avoid that.

Even the ultimate tendency of Ibsen's drama might be taken as Wagnerian. There are suggestions about heroism, about the necessary destructiveness of the will, about the working-out of forces which negate the individual but also usher in a higher form of life—and these are presumably derived from a tendency, a climate of opinion, in the German intellectual world. They go well with the idea of a dramatic form which is itself a large system with internal resonances and consistencies, also working itself out in a way which is larger than the way of the individual will. An examination of the creative, yet also destructive impact of love, breaking open an established personality, moving it into another phase, and then being left behind by that same further-evolving personality—there is another link.

These notions of form, these themes, are only interesting as they are put into practice—as they become music or words, played and sung or acted in the theatre. The similarities between Wagner and Ibsen are at this level of abstractness. Comparison is complicated first by the limitations of the analogy between music drama and spoken drama, where I have suggested that it is mistaken to say that one is inherently better than another. It is complicated further by the judgement that Wagner is a genius of the first order, even if you come to dislike him; while Ibsen is to my mind of the second or third order even in his own sphere, spoken drama—so, in his way, Wagner is better than Ibsen in his. And then I believe that Ibsen has been inflated as a kind of answer to Wagner, or at any rate because people wished to go on believing that a poetic drama was still possible, and that he had found a way back to it. Finally this can only be argued, one way or the other, from a direct inspection of the fine detail of the Norwegian original.

The argument comes back to language, always. It is getting a little awkward to go on saying this: the notion that 'it is all in the language' is becoming an Indian rope-trick in all discussions, about literature, about philosophy, about almost everything. Uttering the

163

phrase, we go swiftly up the rope and disappear. A kindly audience expects the process, and may not press the performer to say too clearly where he is going and how he gets there, or whether he *is* there.

Literary history has had a number of resources. At the simplest level you just say what came after what. Thus there was a renaissance drama, an observable hiatus, then a period of neo-classicism, then the romantic movement. Pressed to say *why*, the historian may resort to 'influence'—either the influence of one writer upon another, or the determining pressures of the time, the so-called *Zeitgeist*. That looks mechanical and determinist, and tends to set up unending chains : why should not the influence itself be determined by another influence, and on the other hand what if some people were resistant to influence? We are currently at the stage where once more we have to grant the autonomy of the writer as an individual with free choice; if nonetheless he is open to 'influences' they must be of a kind which he can hardly evade and may not be conscious of. The language which he uses as instrument, the terms and forms it provides, are things most likely to seem like part of nature. They are also the things that the great innovative genius is most likely to move forward : so 'language as influence' gives a good balance of freedom and constraint.

If you consider romantic literature as a whole, in England, France, and Germany in the nineteenth century, you do have to take note of striking innovatory geniuses at work. Indeed the nineteenth century is the one other period in which language is being used by the writers in ways which seem to have a power of the same general kind as Shakepeare's or Racine's. But it is not being used in the service of drama. The great poets are lyric or reflective writers. The talent which used to go into the drama—the interest in the interaction of selves, or the development of an imagined self working its way out in a lifetime of self-realization or frustration—that talent now expresses itself in the novel. The two interests are in danger of splitting apart, and the exploratory metaphorical power of language, used as an instrument of self-discovery, is in danger of turning into private reverie. It had been the medium of soliloquy in drama, and is now soliloquy in another sense. The solitary writer, silently conceiving it, commits it to paper; the reader, silently repeating it in his solitary reading, undergoes a related experience. This *is* a kind of drama : but that of the silent evolution of mental states. In instrumental music, it is rather like the piano sonata after Beethoven. The composer, alone at his piano, works out a complex form which embodies some kind of evolution or exploration which bears an undoubted relationship to his own emotional process. The reader has to be a performer; alone at *his* piano, he learns to recreate this work, in which he participates in the composer's discoveries. He may then perform the work in public : but he doesn't have to, since it is essentially a self-communing form, overheard by others. Romantic poetry, on the other hand, while it too may be read aloud and in that sense performed, is really aimed direct at the silent solitary reader, and appeals to him as single being. The literary art which deals with the human world, which appeals to him as social being, which satisfies the narrative interest, which deals with human interaction or struggle—that art is now the novel.

For instance, if one were to look back at Macbeth's invocation 'Come, seeling night . . .' (p. 47) and to ask, where in the nineteenth century equivalents of that theme and that richness of evocative power were to be found? answers propose themselves quite quickly. Macbeth is looking out into a darkening world, and seeing in the 'thickening' light and the other circumstances of the time and place a set of meanings—meaning for him. Characteristically he is receiving more than he is willing to be fully conscious of, and so tells us something about himself. That tendency of the self-communing sensibility to look at the landscape, the universe, for auguries or confirmations or inklings is romantic as well. The romantic poet at his most typical is alone, in a landscape. He ponders it, awaiting a message; perhaps some change in the world outside—a wind, a cloud-shadow, a storm, a sunset—takes place, and as he attends the event, something homologous takes place in him and he makes a joint meaning of the associated processes. Seeming to describe the world, he describes himself. At the crude level of response, this is called the 'pathetic fallacy'; and it is thought that romantic poets, being rather stupid and very self-centred, assumed that the universe understands or reciprocates their feelings. Not at all : the poet watches, or feels what takes place out there; and his words for that process become words for an echo in him, a meaning that he is finding.

That kind of poetry too has its primitive stage : in much of Byron or Lamartine it is no more than solemn attitudinizing against a scenic backdrop. But from the beginning, as in Hölderlin or Wordsworth, it could be much more subtle than that : in the third quarter of the nineteenth century, when romantic poetic drama was visibly a lost cause, one finds in France especially, in the poetry of Baudelaire and Mallarmé, but also in England in the extraordinary art of Gerard Manley Hopkins, a final stage of the romantic 'nature poem' in which the poet is the silent focus of a cosmic drama. Hopkins's 'Spelt from Sybil's Leaves', for instance, is a sonnet, though almost unrecognizable as such. It records the onset of night, seen as a process which overarches the sky from one horizon to another. The perception induces anguish in the watching consciousness, because it is seen as a parable of moral night, where easy daylight distinctions are swallowed up. Deprived of light, deprived of measure and certainty, consciousness is a prey to its own tendency to disintegration or self-conflict.

Very similar are certain of Mallarmé's sonnets. He too saw the daily loss of the sun as a repeated drama on the largest scale we can actually witness : he too saw it as inducing an agony of consciousness. In both Hopkins and Mallarmé the poem has become a device of such complexity that fourteen lines are almost all we can be expected to take at a time. It takes hours to decipher them : recitation in a theatre to an audience would be absurd. The texture is so dense and the language so deflected from normal uses that the poems are like verbal objects, which can be turned over and pondered almost as a physical thing. The romantic organic form, the system, has become an algorithm, a discovery-procedure : it is not an instrumental, but a reflexive algorithm, in that what you discover is how to discover—how to read the poem itself. The mind has to submit patiently to the procedures of the poem and learn them as you learn a language : by speaking and repetition. It must be supple enough to be passed through this almost-machine, and take the impress of this deeply calculated set of experiences. The 'meaning' is the experience : and once again, it can be paraphrased, but the paraphrase is not the experience. We are again close to Mendelssohn's insight into the nature of music, and it becomes clear that the apex of the romantic achievement in poetry is once more a music of words. Because what is involved is also a process, in which the reader is meant to follow a mental evolution which replicates the author's procession of ever-deeper insights, this is the kind of solipsist drama in which the romantic tendency to withdraw from the theatre is completed. An ideal drama now takes place when a reader, imagined in a circle of lamplight, alone at night with his book, turns his gaze upon the silent page, with its black marks upon white space. His outward movement of focused attention causes the words to speak in his mind; as they speak they produce not just mental sounds but mental activity. Rhythm will succeed and modify rhythm, theme will respond to theme. An adequate poetry will produce a complexity of symphonic power and extent, of the kind Keats predicted:

> Heard melodies are sweet, but those unheard
> Are sweeter; therefore, ye soft pipes, play on;
> Not to the sensual ear, but, more endeared,
> Pipe to the spirit ditties of no tone . . .

Hopkins was isolated and unknown—a silent figure deliberately severed from the literary life of his time by his vocation and his secretiveness. He had to be discovered long after his death. Mallarmé is therefore in some senses the representative European poet of his generation : the most conscious and reflective; the one most concerned to place what he was doing, to make the right claims for it, and specifically to face the challenge of music and music drama. These were now likely to be considered as the highest arts, in the sense that they were the best representation of the finest consciousness of their time, capable of being represented in the way that Schopenhauer represented music. By extension, music drama, and in particular Wagner's, could claim to have taken the place of poetic drama. Music itself needed no translation—expressly rebuffed it in Mendelssohn's words. The music was its own meaning; you neither needed to convert it into Mendelssohn's German nor any other language : so it was international. Wagner's words were German, but the music supplied the only transposition that was possible, and that too needed no translation. Music in the later nineteenth century had become as much 'used', as much 'consumed', as poetry. After Byron there were only two great popular poets, Tennyson and Hugo, who had a kind of institutional status and value. The enormously successful writers, commercially, were novelists—especially Dickens. The novel as popular form undoubtedly sapped the drama, since like lyric poetry it too appealed to the solitary silent reader, even if there was one or more such readers in hundreds of thousands of homes.

Drama is the public form of literature; it had once been the dominant form of literature and the dominant art. It was becoming a minor form of literature, almost a dying form, certainly not the form that the best writers naturally adopted. The public art, that which assembled together large audiences and submitted them to a common simultaneous experience, in which their being an audience was a powerful element of the experience—this was now music. Or if it is insisted that the popular theatre of the city suburbs and working-class quarters remained vigorous in the late nineteenth century and beyond, then the public art which manifested the *highest* form of consciousness was undoubtedly the music drama. An apt representation of that relationship is the process by which Maeterlinck, attempting a symbolic drama, produced at first the play in prose *Pelléas et Mélisande*. This etiolated work has no force in itself : but Debussy took it, and set it to music without changing a word. So set, it is a powerful drama; if it has defects, they are the defects of the basic play; where it has virtues, they are those of the music.

As poet, critic and theatre-goer, Mallarmé contemplated this virtual crisis. He started from the position that the theatre itself was, by his standards, decadent or insignificant. He saw art nonetheless as a rite of civilization : the representation which took place when a performer appeared before any kind of audience in a formal context and mediated to that audience a set of words or actions prescribed by a written text. This is a religion of art : the supreme rite or performance would be the Mass itself. But if the old religion is not held, then the only way of conveying to an otherwise derelict community the same representation of the ideal is a high art which is capable of bearing the same weight of significance : of interpreting the world, of assigning meaning. The supreme forms of art do this, but humble analogues can also be found, and private ones. Mallarmé found a weight of significance in the idea of the book : the folded sheet of paper with black marks on its whiteness. Unfolded, the sheets are wings, the black marks take off, in a mental flight, like birds— they aim towards the mental or spiritual realm, the ideal. So a man reading a newspaper on a park bench was not a trivial sight for Mallarmé : still less the lecturer (even the academic lecturer) who comes on to a platform, salutes his audience, takes out his notes, sits down at a table, reads or orates, gets up, salutes his audience and

168

leaves. That too is a rite. Highest of all would be a verbal art which took place in a theatre envisaged as a secular temple. Here at stated hours on stated days an audience converges, seriously intent on art; that is to say on participating in a transformatory process in which ordinary persons in greasepaint and costume, between a flaring light and a flat deceptive scene-painting, make rehearsed movements and utter remembered words : and by their public art give the audience an enhanced sense of life and the world.

It had been done, but was not being done. There was a classic drama; there was an abortive romantic drama; there was Scribe (supreme representative of the popular, successful, realistic, and banal); there were attempts at a poetic revival. They did not represent a living art. Meanwhile there was also ballet, a valuable art which did not use words; there was opera, which did. Above all, there was Wagner, who had consciously taken the old despised theatre, and the vulgar successful Grand Opera, appropriated the one, and turned the other into the kind of living art Mallarmé desiderated. Did one have to concede that music and music drama had entirely supplanted poetry and poetic drama?

Wagner came to Paris in the 1860s, as Cavalli had come to Paris in the 1660s. Opera, the new art form in the era of Corneille, Molière and Racine, could be given a tolerant reception by writers conscious of exercising the major art. There was the added interest that Racine in particular was attempting a form of classical tragedy, using classical themes, and could not escape the comparison with the Greeks. Given that the antique chorus had used music and dance, it was 'interesting' that a music drama was being revived. To a severe taste, especially one unfamiliar with Monteverdi's *Orfeo*, the competition was not serious. What Quinault and Lully achieved in collaboration was in a mixed mode, was mostly spectacle, and devalued myth.

A much more serious convergence of the arts was effected in Racine's own *Athalie*, where the heart of Christian myth was represented, where the chorus between the acts offered a functional and expressive comment on the action, so producing a genuinely continuous, seamless whole. The point of the Old Testament story is that the line from which the Redeemer is destined to spring has as its sole representative the child Joas, hidden in the Temple of Jerusalem by the High Priest Joad (Jehoiadah). The child's life is

169

threatened by the tyrannical and unbelieving Queen Athalie, another of Racine's formidable yet vulnerable women. She is tricked into the Temple by Joad and murdered, and the emotional spring which brings her to her death is an almost maternal attachment to the child. So a ruthless God uses what is best and most human in her to destroy her and achieve His purpose. He actually speaks oracularly through the mouth of Joad, and prophesies that the child he is now saving will later be corrupted and die, but meanwhile God's immediate purpose is secured. It is a grim religion, giving an entirely new sense to the phrase that God is love; but then love in Racine's drama is always a scourge. The unities of time and place are naturally and thrillingly observed; the choruses between the acts provide a continuum, an interlude in the exact sense of the word : so the time taken to play the drama is exactly the same as the time taken by the action. The only possible criticism of the play is that the music provided for the chorus to sing by his contemporary Moreau is incomparably less fine than the words. This leaves the words in a position of undoubted dominance. Racine has at last used music, after writing plays with quasi-musical expressive elements in the words; but the music is not his equal. The experiment showed that music was a possible adjunct, but not essential to his drama, which resided in the poetry.

When Wagner came to Paris and *Tannhäuser* was a fiasco, Baudelaire sent him a generous letter of admiration, and wrote an important article about the event. What interested Baudelaire was that this music seemed to do without words what poets did with words : to create in the hearer an intended complex effect. It was the orchestral interludes that Baudelaire was interested in, and he quoted the reactions of distinguished hearers, who listening to this music with their eyes shut, were able to report reactions with important areas of conceptual overlap, even though there were discrepancies in their figurative paraphrases of the kind of scene intended. They all had a sense of the ethereal, the spiritual, the transformatory power of something not human reaching out (or rather down) to a human consciousness. Baudelaire wrote as colleague in another art, trying to operate through words alone related transformations in the consciousness of his readers. He had no sense of rivalry or threat, in fact he could afford to be generous to an artist who had suffered a rebuff which discredited the intelligence of France.

By Mallarmé's time, the relationship had decisively changed. Wagner had colossally succeeded in a way Mallarmé could not hope to do : had had exalted sponsorship of an effective kind, had acquired a kind of shrine in Bayreuth, had large and regular audiences, had —in short—imposed his vision and his art in a way which only 'commercial' artists now normally managed.

Asked therefore to write something for the *Revue Wagnérienne* of January 1886 as a tribute to the now dead Wagner, Mallarmé produced his cryptic *Hommage*, one of his most obscure sonnets. It starts, probably, from the observation that most nineteenth-century theatres have a classical portico with pillars and pediment. The suggestion of a temple-tomb provides a direct visual analogy with the shrine of a god. First he evoked the mausoleum, the silence and mourning, the black hangings, immediately following a death. But the temple-tomb is at the end of the poem transformed back into a theatre; silence, mourning, and oblivion are transformed into rejoicing and fame. What operates the transformation is the rite performed every time one of the works of the dead man is performed; he is then reborn in glory as 'the god Richard Wagner'—and this is the modern equivalent of the antique apotheosis (the word 'god' is not lightly used).

The verbal structure works through this transformation of opposites : shrine into theatre, black into gold, silence into triumph, an orchestrated chaos into the dominance of a master-theme on the trumpets; the black marks of the notated score into the synaesthetic polychrome of the performed music. Beneath these contrasts is another, an anxious one. Does this new art invalidate old ones, as the new theatrical form devalues the old theatre? In particular, is Wagner's music, in ambition the complete art-form, a more perfect —*the* perfect—expression of what poets had been trying to do with words only? Has the book, the play, ceded primacy to the score? Is this, in short, not just *a* rite of civilization but *the* rite?

The implied answer is no; for Mallarmé is subtly and slily pointing out that he too can do all this—he can make music's claim—in words. He has just operated in this mere 14 lines a staggering set of transformations, conveyed by his figurative polyphony. He has met Wagner on his own ground, and his tribute of mourning does not conceal the poet's own claim.

It is a lot to hang on 14 lines : but then Mallarmé's words are

171

given their force by being part of a total output in which the sense of a sonnet is not easily discoverable, except by knowing all that Mallarmé meant to mean, and to know *that* you have to read and ponder the whole work. His was an important labour; but when you have reached some understanding of it, it is borne in on you to what extent these are the exceedingly refined thoughts of a mind so far removed from the business of everyday that the predicament of the subtle writer, his remoteness from the man in the street, has been turned into a redoubt, a fortification. You have to fight your way in.

The man in the street may not hum very much Wagner, but the man in the opera house does. When all is said and done, Wagner had a currency, and still does, that Mallarmé did not and will not have. It springs not only from Wagner's own genius. It has something important to do with the nature of the art he practised. Music, we are reminded again, needs no translation and for most ordinary hearers no commentary. Music in the theatre links the universal language to a communal or popular art. It aims to have a currency and breadth of appeal that Mallarmé's poetry consciously avoided; and could not have secured if it had wanted it.

If you go into a large metropolitan opera house on a special occasion, and look at the patrons, you may if you have a puritan turn of mind be discouraged. Most of these expensively dressed or undressed people are there to see each other and be seen; the music, the drama, is only the occasion for their dressing, dining and being togther. If you go on an ordinary night to a municipal opera house in a middle-sized European city, especially in the German-speaking countries, you will see a great deal more seriousness about the art. But even that is a little equivocal. At the interval soberly dressed middle-aged middle-class people walk round and round in the areas of the theatre provided for people to walk round and round in; and this begins to look like the other serious business of the evening. They eye each other without too obviously doing so and estimate prosperity, health and age; or they exchange greetings with people they know. Daughters, too, are there to be seen, looking demure and marriageable, and sons no doubt see them. Various social purposes are being accomplished by evenings at the *Städtische Bühnen*, as they are by an evening at Covent Garden or the Met.

172

So they should be. That is what theatres are for, in addition to the art. If people have mixed motives in this matter, it is because they have mixed motives in all others too. It is a strength of the theatre that it has unconscious functions which make it a vigorous organ of a community as well as a stage for an art. Making all due allowances, the opera now, rather than the theatre, serves the artistic and social functions once served in England, Spain and France by a poetic drama. If we are ever to have an effective poetic drama again it might conceivably happen when dramatic poets collaborate with musicians, and so reconquer a willing audience as Hofmannsthal did with Strauss. (May any future poet as good as Hofmannsthal find a composer better than Strauss, one says to oneself, over-fastidiously. But opera is a strong, even a coarse art. A Strauss can find a place in it, especially when he is helped by a Hoffmansthal.) If people put up with opera for the sake of the occasion, some of them discover a taste; they might put up with poets for the sake of the music and discover another depth. They might find, as people always do, I believe, that what they had taken for a distraction is an art, and important to them.

Appendix

Expressive Elements in Racine's Verse

Considered as an ideal abstraction, the French heroic couplet is simply two Alexandrines linked by a rhyme. Two lines of twelve syllables each contain six feet of two syllables. Notionally, there is a pause in the middle of each line, the caesura, which is like a breath. So we have four half-lines, each of six syllables, which can be thought of musically as four phrases of three measures each, the second and fourth ending in a rhyme, which is like a harmonic linking-device.

In fact, because it is put to expressive use, and the use has effects on the internal structure of the form, the 'pure' alexandrine is rarely heard. The expressive purpose is always producing some stress, some rhythmic pressure, which produces an intensification. For instance, Phèdre's own first lines :

> N'allons point plus avant. Demeurons, chère Oenone.
> Je ne me soutiens plus, ma force m'abandonne.

These use the broken measure of the end-stopped line, with pause and punctuation at the half-line as well. This is not a neutral, but an expressive use. Phèdre's fever and giddiness are not merely in the mind; it is a real bodily decrepitude. She cannot walk more than a few steps; she cannot breathe out more than a half-line at a time.

In itself, the couplet-form tends naturally to concision, invites epigram. Its duple nature expresses itself naturally as antithesis. Hence some telling utterances, for instance :

> Quand tu sauras mon crime, et le sort qui m'accable
> Je n'en mourrai pas moins, j'en mourrai plus coupable.

Here again are four equal half-lines, now positive and grim. Parallels instantly come to mind, for instance the equally sad and bitter words of Phèdre to Hippolyte :

175

De quoi m'ont profité mes inutiles soins?
Tu me haïssais plus, je ne t'aimais pas moins.

These balances (*plus ... moins*) give the line an undulant movement; not just a musical see-saw, but a sober weighing, with sadness as the balance comes finally down against the speaker. Contrast those lines where *dernière* comes out with even greater force, sounding disturbingly like an arrival home, to death :

Soleil, je te viens voir pour la dernière fois.

or

Je péris la dernière, et la plus misérable.

A device which Racine often uses as an expository technique is the couplet in which a ringing half-line is confidently thrown out, and then followed by an amplificatory line-and-a-half which has the effect of undermining the confidence. *Phèdre* begins with one :

Hippolyte : Le dessein en est pris : je pars, cher Théramène;
Et quitte le séjour de l'aimable Trézène ...

After a time one learns to look on the second line-and-a-half as holding the reason why one should discount the confidence of the first half. We learn in this case that *l'aimable Trézène* is being left because it harbours a threat to Hippolyte's peace of mind, and *that* is why, after six months' inaction, he is now busy about his father's fate.

Musically, however, the half-line gets the scene instantly into motion with a strong phrase, and the immediate modulation away in rapid rhythm carries the interest along on an exciting arioso.

The current can be cut across, however, or diverted; and here rhyme is a powerful device, the equivalent of an unexpected interval or harmony. Consider, for instance, at the end of a long earnest speech, Hippolyte's

... Et dans un fol amour ma jeunesse embarquée ... ?
Théramène : Ah, Seigneur, si votre heure est une fois marquée,
Le ciel de nos raisons ne sait point s'informer.

The busy self-justifying arguments are cut through by Théramène's ironic slower movement, and the strong rhyme clinches the rebuttal. Or in the same scene, Théramène's gentle and respectful but nonetheless taunting line is turned away by Hippolyte's brusque one : a curiously satisfying use of the couplet, where the rhyme reminds one of the poetic unit, but everything else tends to break it down :

Théramène : La charmante Aricie a-t-elle su vous plaire?
Hippolyte : Théramène, je pars, et vais chercher mon père.

That kind of fracture, an intense disappointment of the expectation aroused by the first line of the couplet, can occur without a change of voice : Hippolyte, urging Aricie to flee with him just before the catastrophe, has a whole 14 powerful, swift lines, urging her very strongly. He begins the eighth couplet confidently :

L'occasion est belle, il la faut embrasser.

Something in her face topples the whole edifice; the expected strong second line splinters into two anxious questions :

Quelle peur vous retient? Vous semblez balancer?

The weak rhyme underlines the collapse.

The placing of the stress, whether on the rhyme or elsewhere, provides a kind of weight which Racine can slide along his line, to make it balance as he wishes. For instance Aricie's words to Thésée :

Prenez garde, Seigneur. Vos invincibles mains
Ont de monstres sans nombre affranchi les humains;
Mais tout n'est pas détruit, et vous en laissez vivre
Un . . .

The introduction of the 'monster' theme, the veiled reference to Phèdre's perfidy, give the lines great weight which is moved along the three lines to hang, enormously, on the single syllable *Un*. She cannot be more explicit, for Hippolyte has enjoined silence on her; but she can with this richly harmonized hint shake Thésée's certainties.

Similarly, Phèdre's

J'aime. Ne pense pas qu'au moment que je t'aime,
Innocente à mes yeux, je m'approuve moi-même.

gives the first syllable the force of a chord. Then the normal rhythm takes up the movement again.

In moments of extreme intensity the measure almost disappears, being broken into agitated phrases :

Oenone : Juste ciel ! tout mon sang dans mes veines se glace.
O désespoir ! O crime ! O déplorable race !
Voyage infortuné ! Rivage malheureux,
Fallait-il approcher de tes bords dangereux ?

(Yet even that little mood-intensifying outburst carries on two main themes.)

Conversely of course, when Phèdre or Thésée is in a towering passion, the melodic line leaps over the couplet-endings in a torrent. For instance, Phèdre's curse on Oenone, a single sentence, a single melodic arch, of eight lines :

Puisse le juste ciel dignement te payer,
Et puisse ton supplice à jamais effrayer
Tous ceux qui, comme toi, par de lâches addresses,
Des princes malheureux nourissent les faiblesses,
Les poussent au penchant où leur coeur est enclin,
Et leur osent du crime aplanir le chemin ;
Détestables flatteurs, présent le plus funeste
Que puisse faire aux rois la colère celeste !

This is one jet, but the rhymes and the pauses give musical control, making it possible to project it with both the force, the unity and the expressive variation in the rhythm which the sense requires.

Another related effect is the frenetic ostinato of the rhyme in the climactic lines of Phèdre's confession to Oenone :

Vaines précautions ! Cruelle destinée !
Par mon époux lui-même à Trézène amenée,
J'ai revu l'ennemi que j'avais éloigné ;
Ma blessure trop vive aussitôt a saigné,
Ce n'est plus une ardeur dans mes veines cachée :
C'est Vénus toute entière à sa proie attachée.

Thésée's tremendous imprecation (cursing Hippolyte) has a splendid rhythm, and a kind of strophic structure which does all the work. There is comparatively little complexity in the details of the language ; though the words tell us a good deal about the speaker :

Perfide, oses-tu bien te montrer devant moi ?
Monstre, qu'a trop longtemps épargné le tonnerre,
Reste impur des brigands dont j'ai purgé la terre.
Après que le transport d'un amour plein d'horreur

Jusqu'au lit de ton père a porté sa fureur,
Tu m'oses présenter une tête ennemie,
Tu parais dans des lieux pleins de ton infamie,
Et ne vas pas chercher, sous un ciel inconnu,
Des pays où mon nom ne soit point parvenu.
Fuis, traître. Ne viens point braver ici ma haine,
Et tenter un courroux que je retiens à peine.
C'est bien assez pour moi de l'opprobre éternel
D'avoir pu mettre au jour un fils si criminel,
Sans que ta mort encor, honteuse à ma mémoire,
Des mes nobles travaux vienne souiller la gloire.
Fuis; et si tu ne veux qu'un châtiment soudain
T'ajoute aux scélérats qu'a punis cette main,
Prends garde que jamais l'astre qui nous éclaire
Ne te voie en ces lieux mettre un pied téméraire.
Fuis, dis-je; et sans retour précipitant tes pas,
De ton horrible aspect purge tous mes Etats.
Et toi, Neptune, et toi, si jadis mon courage
D'infames assassins nettoya ton rivage,
Souviens-toi que pour prix de mes efforts heureux,
Tu promis d'exaucer le premier de mes voeux.
Dans les longues rigueurs d'une prison cruelle
Je n'ai point imploré ta puissance immortelle.
Avare du secours que j'attends de tes soins,
Mes voeux t'ont réservé pour de plus grands besoins :
Je t'implore aujourd'hui. Venge un malheureux père.
J'abandonne ce traître à toute ta colère;
Etouffe dans son sang ses désirs effrontés :
Thésée à tes fureurs connaîtra tes bontés.

The first line, in a blast of hate, shrivels the courteous olive branch offered by Hippolyte (*N'osez vous confier ce secret à ma foi?*). There follow eight lines which turn on Hippolyte the 'monster' theme, and which drive angrily across the couplet-endings in a single sense and melodic unit. The speech then falls into two great strophes of twelve lines. The first falls naturally into two groups of six, each prefaced *Fuis* . . . and in the last couplet this *Fuis* is repeated, in a sort of coda. One imagines the word repeated on a rising scale.

In the second strophe Thésée takes breath and winds himself up to the curse. His *Et toi, Neptune, et toi* . . . shows him, hands raised, stretching himself to this enormity. There are three quatrains of increasing intensity, in which the curse itself is held back to the end.

In the last four lines it comes out like an arrow, on the highest note of all :

> Je t'implore aujourd'hui. Venge un malheureux père.

The last lines are pure savagery, with a final contorted antithesis :

> Etouffe dans son sang ses désirs effrontés
> Thésée à tes fureurs connaîtra tes bontés.

The first line of the couplet, with its fiercely mouthed consonants, its frothing f's, hints at a horrible satisfaction in Thésée. It also links back with a line in the first scene, where Hippolyte, speaking with pride of Thésée, had mentioned

> Les monstres étouffés et les brigands punis.

Hippolyte is now to be the last such monster, as Thésée himself has made clear. The last line, with its *pointe*, brings the whole aria to a crashing climax. But the harmony has a sinister dissonance; it looks forward to the moment when Thésée's curse is fulfilled at the very moment when he wishes to unsay it, and he then has to admit that

> Je hais jusques au soin dont m'honorent les Dieux;
> Et je m'en vais pleurer leurs faveurs meurtrières,
> Sans plus les fatiguer d'inutiles prières.

It is an awful irony that he is now uttering with such primitive satisfaction.

Several of the passages quoted here contain an obvious intensificatory device, repetition. When a composer is setting words and there is a disparity between the shape of his melodic measure and the natural phrasing of the words, he may either trope the words or use repetition. If the repetition comes at a significant point melodically and rhythmically, it intensifies the utterance. It can become a weak device, a *cheville* or mere filler, and like alliteration it has no intrinsic significance or statutory meaning; but it can accentuate whatever is being expressed. For instance, Aricie, learning of Hippolyte's love, is overcome :

> De tout ce que j'entends étonnée et confuse,
> Je crains presque, je crains qu'un songe ne m'abuse.
> Veillé-je? Puis-je croire un semblable dessein?
> Quel dieu, Seigneur, quel dieu l'a mis dans votre sein?

That is a compound repetition : the fourth line repeating the form of the second : so it is like a strophe in a song. It is attractively rhythmical, in a delicate breathless way.

One can have the effect of repetition without actually repeating the words, as in Phèdre's

> J'ai langui, j'ai séché, dans les feux, dans les larmes . . .

Here the effect is entirely in the movement : a bitter reminiscence, where the swings of the verse mirror the swings of her mood in a self-frustrating turmoil.

I mention below Aricie's curious triumphs, as in :

> Mes yeux alors, mes yeux n'avaient pas vu son fils

or

> C'est là ce que je veux, c'est là ce qui m'irrite;

And there is Phèdre's hallucination of love in the labyrinth :

> C'est moi, Prince, c'est moi, dont l'utile secours
> Vous eût du labyrinthe enseigné les détours.

The language of these phrases is often strikingly simple : the directness of utterance in these intense moments derives from the basic ego, which often sounds child-like (though not innocent).

The vocal music of the time is particularly rich in word-painting. One can hear the composers rising with pleasure to ingenious solutions of the problem of suiting the melodic line and the rhythmic pressure to the sense of the words, in order to produce, by this aptness, an intensification. This goes well beyond simple onomatopoeia or analogical movement to the more subtle, though still very direct, devices of 'affectiveness' : thus, from within the words, to produce, inevitably, something like an actor's expressive declamation. Few composers of the time were given words which offered an equivalent to their own skills, or a proper challenge. But the paradox of this investigation is that as soon as the words reach that degree of organization they no longer need the music.

When Phèdre says

> Tout m'afflige et me nuit et conspire à me nuire

her high thin i-sounds provide exactly the whimper of despair, like a child in a fever, that Racine wants. When she thinks, meltingly, of her abandoned sister, her

181

> Ariane, ma soeur ! de quelle amour blessée
> Vous mourûtes aux bords où vous fûtes laisée !

leaves nothing for the flutes to add.

Or, on the other hand, when the naked ego is exposed, the formal manner dropped, in

> Ah ! cruel, tu m'as trop entendue.
> Je t'en ai dit assez pour te tirer d'erreur,

one hears two things : the *tutoiement*, where all before had been *Prince* and *Seigneur*, but still more the hail of t's and d's, from bared teeth, expressing her complicated scorn and anger. A similar effect is created by Thésée's :

> Le perfide ! Il n'a pu s'empécher de pâlir !

But of course the device itself can suit every purpose. Compare the directly opposite effect in Phèdre's

> Mais fidèle, mais fier, et même un peu farouche.

(Beneath the suave alliteration there is a covert reference to the 'wild' animal theme.)

When Théramène enters, very near the end, in his tremendous *récit* to recount the death of Hippolyte, he has by his words alone to create the excitement, the fear, the final horror of the whole catastrophe. Only something near music can, over that great expanse of narrative, give the sense of involvement without which, at this crucial moment, the whole tragedy can fall into a flat police-court witness's tale of an unfortunate accident. What is more, the narrative has to make the monster sound plausible. It is at least kept off the stage, unlike the operatic monsters which it engendered, but can it be made really horrible? All Racine's vocal and orchestral powers are needed.

Théramène begins with a low, sober, pulsing movement : his drums (as it were) keeping pace with the troop setting out from the city :

> A peine nous sortions des portes de Trézène,
> Il était sur son char. Ses gardes affligés
> Imitaient son silence, autour de lui rangés ;
> Il suivait tout pensif le chemin de Mycènes ;
> Sa main sur ses chevaux laissait flotter les rênes.

The tone is low and uneasy. The short phrases of the second and third lines give an anxious movement. The melody moves into the hunter-Neptune-horsemanship motives, but it moves back into the minor after a brief opening-out :

> Ses superbes coursiers, qu'on voyait autrefois
> Pleins d'une ardeur si noble obéir à sa voix,
> L'oeil morne maintenant et la tête baissée,
> Semblaient se conformer à sa triste pensée.

Then the pace quickens, and the 'monster' theme now has its most portentous entry : all the preoccupations contained in the theme are now incarnated in an actual great beast, announced with a terrible antiphon. The voices rises urgently :

> Un effroyable cri, sorti du fond des flots,
> Des airs en ce moment a troublé le repos ;
> Et du sein de la terre une voix formidable
> Répond en gémissant à ce cri redoutable.

Heaven and earth have cried out against some pollution.

I need not go on, beyond saying that the speech contains the touches of art which sustain its function. Consider for instance, as the monster beaches,

> Le flot qui l'apporta recule épouvanté.

The line rolls up to the caesura with a little breaking sound, and sinks back, hushed. The simplicity of the screech and snap of

> L'essieu crie et se rompt.

is wonderfully effective and direct. Much more subtle is the line describing the monster :

> Sa croupe se recourbe en replis tortueux.

One feels that at first as difficult consonantal activity in the mouth, curiously energetic. Then one sees that *Sa* is transforming itself into *se*, *croupe* into *-courbe* into *recourbe* into *replis*. The whole slithering peristalsis is contained in those elegant, almost surreptitious effects.

These are subtle touches, to the extent that the robust hearer may dismiss them as nonsense, and 'subjective'. My next examples are perhaps even more so, but I ask the reader to listen and feel. Aricie, proud and lonely like Hippolyte, has fallen violently in love with him, though his father Thésée, her captor, is determined that she should marry no-one. She tells Ismène :

> Je rendais souvent grace à l'injuste Thésée
> Dont l'heureuse rigueur secondait mes mepris.

Then, it seems to me, a brightness comes into her eye : she cannot restrain it :

> Mes yeux alors, mes yeux n'avaient pas vu son fils.

I think there is an audible hiss of involvement there, of quite a complicated kind. She goes on, scorning conventional loves,

> Non que par ses yeux seuls lâchement enchantée,
> J'aime en lui sa beauté, sa grâce tant vantée . . .

As she brushes the gifts aside, I seem to hear a certain salivation in *lâchement enchantée* (*lâche* is always a charged word for Racine). She goes on, giving herself away more and more, and revealing (to me at any rate) a disturbingly predatory nature. Her speech reaches what I can only call a climax (meaning just that) :

> Pour moi, je suis plus fière, et fuis la gloire aisée
> D'arracher un hommage à mille autres offert,
> Et d'entrer dans un coeur de toutes parts ouvert.

(There is real scorn there for the old philanderer Thésée.) The other note is heard again :

> Mais de faire fléchir un courage inflexible,
> De porter la douleur dans une âme insensible,
> D'enchaîner un captif de ses fers étonné,
> Contre un joug qui lui plaît vainement mutiné :
> C'est là ce que je veux, c'est là ce qui m'irrite.
> Hercule à désarmer coûtait moins qu'Hippolyte,
> Et vaincu plus souvent, et plus tôt surmonté
> Préparait moins de gloire aux yeux qui l'ont dompté.

The images link, of course, with those used later by Hippolyte, when he confesses his love. He *is* tamed; he has felt the yoke. Here, Aricie's salivating ch's and g's and j's (if I can put it that way) carry on from the hiss in *Mes yeux alors, mes yeux* . . . There is the same excited repetition (*c'est là ce que je veux, c'est là* . . .) in curiously childlike language. There is the odd word *irrite*, used twice in the play, and

184

both times conveniently rhyming with *Hippolyte*, so, useful in that sense and not necessarily having a sexual meaning, and yet it produces a quite specific sound in the throat. Anyway the last three lines are open-throated triumph, and a kind of nakedness (and in *dompté* a modulation into the animal imagery).

This vein of languorous, or intense, or openly climactic erotic expression is sufficiently familiar in the music of the time. Monteverdi's settings of hymns to the Virgin had used it quite freely; so too did Purcell's settings of portions of the Song of Songs, which use a kind of expressiveness which could be even more freely indulged in secular dramatic songs. Indeed it is a more or less universal idiom of the age : a complex, one might say, which is variously audible in Crashaw, Donne and Herbert, and has as its icon Bernini's statue of St Theresa. The spectators saw the point (which is not 'explained', but made crude, by Freudian concepts).

I shall be allowed the other instance of this particular effect. At any rate, I am not the first to see it. It emerges almost grotesquely in Robert Lowell's translation of the passage. Indeed I would say he makes it over-explicit and disconcertingly jaunty. Phèdre, having admitted her love to Hippolyte and finding him horrified, is in an agony of shame. She begs him to kill her, but in her exasperated state the anticipated pleasure of death is mingled with her feelings of love : this is now the only way he could be willing to pleasure her. We break into her tortured utterance at the monster theme :

> Délivre l'unvers d'un monstre qui l'irrite.
> La veuve de Thésée ose aimer Hippolyte !
> Crois-moi, ce monstre affreux ne doit point t'échapper.
> Voilà mon coeur. C'est là que ta main doit frapper.
> Impatient déjà d'expier son offense,
> Au devant de ton bras je le sens qui s'avance.
> Frappe. Ou si tu le crois indigne de tes coups,
> Si ta haine m'envie un supplice si doux,
> Ou si d'un sang trop vil ta main serait trempée,
> Au défaut de ton bras prête-moi ton épée.
> Donne.

It is a wonderful complexity : the insight into the turmoil of the feelings is matched by the awful skill with which the movement and the music do the trick. The spun-out sentence (*Impatient déjà . . .*) which she breathes out, ending *Frappe*; the even longer sentence

185

with its four heaving movements (*Ou si . . . , si . . . , ou si . . . , au défaut . . .*) and the internal assonance *supplice si doux*; at the end of all this the gasped-out *Donne* is a plea for a sexual release; at the moment when it is imminent. The shame of this complicated public humiliation is one trigger of the tragedy. Nobody could have a thing like that burst out of them without questioning in utter horror their own responsibility (assuming that they could recover their equilibrium sufficiently to reflect about it at all). This is the monstrous part of love, which subdues the will, the intelligence, even the most basic social inhibitions. The figure of the monster is not a mere conventional allusion, but a key to the play.

This kind of detailed analysis is revealing but disintegrative, suggesting that Racine wrote in fine lines or fine couplets or the occasional fine speech. That is misleading. I now analyse a long passage of dialogue in order to show how the music is a continuous medium : offering development, contrast, harmonic enrichment—an art which is in fact strikingly like that of the operatic composer.

The passage is from Act I Scene iii of *Phèdre*. One ought to quote and analyse the entire scene, which is musically a unity; space forbids, but I think I can in some 50 lines isolate a succession of movements.

Phèdre has appeared on stage for the first time, after a scene of exposition in which her ill-fated ancestry, her apparent hostility to her stepson Hippolyte, her mysterious malady, have been introduced as themes (*sang*; *haine*—with an implied paradoxical relationship with *amour*; *mal*). She seems fevered and broken. In the early part of this scene she speaks slowly and against her will, in a dark minor key; rather briefly (never more than two couplets). Thematically, her speeches have touched on her fever, on the dazzling light she has sought and cannot now bear, on her affliction which seems like a persecution from without; on her ancestry again (her descent from the sun-god, source of light, witness of her guilt—and here three themes coalesce). There are three reverberant lines in which she feels a pang of longing for the coolness and shade of the forest (a rich theme, which links with the numerous references in the play to Hippolyte as hunter, as himself a free wild young animal to be hunted and tamed; with associations of youth, escape, innocence and sexual fulfilment). Indeed, a betraying reference to the obsessive love for

Hippolyte (merely hinted at as the unnamed occupant of a chariot
fleeing from her in a cloud of 'noble dust') escapes her. At once she
becomes more voluble, in six quick lines which draw the spectator's
attention to her lapse and her shame. But Oenone, her nurse and
confidante, fails to notice this, so busily is she maintaining a steady
vehement pressure on Phèdre to do just that : to explain her malady.
But Phèdre resists; she must; because to reveal her guilty longing
would mean she must then kill herself. So Oenone, urging Phèdre
back to life, is endangering her life. If Phèdre can remain silent, she
may survive. But a specific reference by Oenone to Hippolyte by
name, like a blow, forces out of Phèdre the gasping

> Malheureuse, quel nom est sorti de ta bouche?

and one can hear the long painful exhalation in *malheureuse*.
Oenone, still not realizing how 'warm' she is, presses her attack; she
has a whole ten energetic lines, ending with a small climax, containing a theme (the flame of life, which is related to the flame of love):

> Réparez promptement votre force abattue
> Tandis que de vos jours, prets à se consumer,
> Le flambeau dure encore, et peut se rallumer.

(and compare the last line of Phèdre's great confession, mentioned
below). I now quote and comment on the next 50 lines; I give them
first uninterrupted because I hope the reader will feel for himself the
rhythm of the whole passage :

Phèdre : J'en ai trop prolongé la coupable durée.	1
Oenone : Quoi? de quelques remords êtes-vous déchirée?	
Quel crime a pu produire un trouble si pressant?	
Vos mains n'ont point trempé dans le sang innocent?	
Phèdre : Graces au ciel, mes mains ne sont point criminelles,	5
Plut aux Dieux que mon coeur fût innocent comme elles !	
Oenone : Et quel affreux projet avez-vous enfanté,	
Dont votre coeur encor doive être épouvanté?	
Phèdre : Je t'en ai dit assez. Epargne-moi le reste.	
Je meurs, pour ne point faire un aveu si funeste.	10
Oenone : Mourez donc, et gardez un silence inhumain;	
Mais pour fermer vos yeux cherchez une autre main.	
Quoiqu'il vous reste à peine une faible lumière,	
Mon âme chez les morts descendra la première.	
Mille chemins ouverts y conduisent toujours,	15

Et ma juste douleur choisira les plus courts.
Cruelle, quand ma foi vous a-t-elle déçue?
Songez-vous qu'en naissant mes bras vous ont reçue?
Mon pays, mes enfants, pour vous j'ai tout quitté.
Réserviez-vous ce prix à ma fidélité?   20
Phèdre : Quel fruit espères-tu de tant de violence?
Tu frémiras d'horreur si je romps le silence.
Oenone : Et que me direz-vous qui ne cède, grands Dieux !
A l'horreur de vous voir expirer à mes yeux?
Phèdre : Quand tu sauras mon crime, et le sort qui m'accable,   25
Je n'en mourrai pas moins, j'en mourrai plus coupable.
Oenone : Madame, au nom des pleurs que pour vous j'ai versés,
Par vos faibles genoux que je tiens embrassés,
Délivrez mon esprit de ce funeste doute.
Phèdre : Tu le veux. Lève-toi.
Oenone :   Parlez : je vous écoute.   30
Phèdre : Ciel ! que lui vais-je dire? Et par où commencer?
Oenone : Par de vaines frayeurs cessez de m'offenser.
Phèdre : O haine de Vénus ! O fatale colère !
Dans quels égarements l'amour jeta ma mère !
Oenone : Oublions-les, Madame. Et qu'à tout l'avenir   35
Un silence éternel cache ce souvenir.
Phèdre : Ariane, ma soeur ! de quel amour blessée,
Vous mourûtes aux bords où vous fûtes laissée !
Oenone : Que faites-vous, Madame? Et quel mortel ennui
Contre tout votre sang vous anime aujourd'hui?   40
Phèdre : Puisque Vénus le veut, de ce sang déplorable
Je péris la dernière, et la plus misérable.
Oenone : Aimez-vous?
Phèdre :   De l'amour j'ai toutes les fureurs.
Oenone : Pour qui?
Phèdre :   Tu vas ouïr le comble des horreurs.
J'aime . . . A ce nom fatal, je tremble, je frissonne.   45
J'aime . . .
Oenone :   Qui?
Phèdre :   Tu connais ce fils de l'Amazone,
Ce prince si longtemps par moi-même opprimé?
Oenone : Hippolyte ! Grands Dieux !
Phèdre :   C'est toi qui l'as nommé.

Phèdre's single line (1) answering Oenone's strongly and simply
rhythmic, pressing attack, is slow and long, partly by natural association with the content ('too long already . . .'). Oenone swings back

with three end-stopped lines, each a hard question (2–4). Her tempo is maintained; the strong rhythms, the emphases (*remords, crime, déchirée, trouble, sang*) which are themselves motives, pile on the pressure. Again Phèdre slows the rhythm with a long sighing couplet (5–6). She raises her hands, perhaps, to the heaven she both invokes and hesitates to attest. The note of mysterious guilt characterizes the itensified tonality. There is an irony here : by the end of the day her hands *will* be bloodstained. Oenone now shortens her measure, and puts all her impetus into a balancing couplet (7–8); still an urgent question, and still pressing hard, insisting on her swift dominant rhythm. And in *enfanté*, linked with *affreux*, she touches lightly on another motive, one of the two major figures of the whole play : the 'monster' theme. Still Phèdre will not pay out more than a couplet (9–10); still she resists the rhythm; with her painful effort of will she holds back both Oenone's curiosity and the fatality she sees behind it. Indeed the strong caesura at the end of the first sentence, corresponding with the formal hemistich; the pause at the end-stopped line; the long sigh of the second line, represent almost a complete halt to the movement of the scene. With *meurs*, and *aveu si funeste*, we reach the painful end of a paragraph. The irony of the line, the insistence that confession brings death (and so it does, in the complicated sequel) bring us to the darkest tonality.

So Oenone goes back, as it were, in a reprise; takes breath and returns to the attack in another powerful speech, of exactly the same length (five couplets) as that which preceded my extract. It is like a repeated strophe; but now she is more bitter, and she plays strongly on her personal hold on Phèdre. There is another irony, a more unforeseen and appalling one, in the prediction about her own death (14–16). The last two couplets, with their three questions (a variation, as it were, on lines 2–4), the bitter claim about her own faithfulness, are meant to shake Phèdre's magnanimity.

Phèdre *is* shaken; but she modulates, in a third decelerating couplet (21–22) back to the awfulness of the consequence. So she carries on her own measure, and the theme and tonality of her last couplet; but the discord is even sharper.

Oenone's answering couplet (23–24) is almost purely formal; its function is partly to take the form (two lines) and return it hard, with maintained intensity and increased tempo. Her single sentence drives across the line-break in a surging rhythm. Its function is also to evoke Phèdre's answering couplet; the unit is maintained, but the overall exchange is halted again; brought to a dead-centre just before an intensifying climax. Lines 25–26 are the most awful of Phèdre's four dark utterances (5–6, 9–10, 21–22, 25–26). It is the 'pure' couplet; end-stopped, with the caesura at the hemistich, the whole sentence strongly antithetical. The formality underlines the importance of the utterance. Like all the ironies in the play, it emphasizes the tightness of the structure and the inevitability of the catastrophe. What she now says will happen, does happen : she is making a right judgement, an oracular prophecy. There is a note of self-loathing which derives from the sense that she is either responsible for her actions and guilty, or not responsible for them and just as guilty but more horrifying (monstrous, in short). Her will is corrupted and about to give way; even the temptation to confess has an attraction. The polarities coalesce about the antithesis in these lines. In their vigour they show great mental lucidity and power of judgement—even a movement towards control—and yet her vision confirms that she will die, and her death will be the more guilty if she cannot hold her tongue. So the structural balance of the verse expresses mental energy and moral clarity, set against hopeless self-condemnation and an impending abdication of the will.

A pause. It is the end of a second movement. The tension is now extremely strong; the key is sombre and menacing. Phèdre's slow couplets have nonetheless held back, so far, Oenone's strong pressures.

Oenone uses her last resource. A gesture now underlines this. She goes down on her knees, clasps Phèdre's in the posture of a suppliant. She goes back to a triple measure (cf. lines 2–4), and in three solemn lines of conjuration presses an appeal which Phèdre as queen, as foster-child, as magnanimous nature, cannot reject.

This is a climax. There is another pause, but a very brief one. The two half-lines which now suggest by a kind of musical punctuation that we have passed from one movement to another are the dramatic equivalent of a perfect cadence. Phèdre's half-line is level, bleak and tough : Oenone's looks forward into the next movement, as if to set a key. The caesura falls between them as if after long opposition, a kind of syncopation, the two voices are now about to move in rhythmic unison. And in simple stage terms, the words enable Oenone to rise to her feet.

Another fractional pause, as the two women face each other. We now expect the confession : will Phèdre launch into an aria? By a triumph of Racine's insight which is also a touch of art, her courage fails. The music has now to go back and wind her up again to the full open-throated pitch. She quails, and her first single line (31) has two functions; to show that her will is not yet gone, or that she has not quite the courage to abandon herself, and in a kind of orchestral tremolando on the low strings, to serve as the base of another passage of mounting tension. A large theme is being heralded. Her single line is returned, a semi-tone higher, by Oenone (32), and the pressure begins to mount again.

Phèdre now returns to her couplet-measure. She speaks the first of another three, all deeply thematic, turning on her fate and the fate of her family, coming steadily forward in time, closer to herself, in a rising scale. The first (33–34) is strong and agitated; the first line broken into two exclamations, announcing the *Vénus* theme, the fatality theme. Oenone's balancing, supporting couplet (35–36) is soothing, hushing : the structure is the same with the first line broken into equal measures. Phèdre's antiphonal couplet (37–38), closer in time, more plangent, more urgent, has the lovely flute-notes about Ariane. The 'death-wounds' of love are thematic. Oenone's reply, warning and questioning, with the same divided first line, carries on the theme of death (*mortel*) and the fatal dynastic note (*sang*). With that phrase already sounded, out comes Phèdre's last, strongest, most desperate couplet (41–42). She has reached herself; *Vénus* and *sang* sound in the same line; and the second one has one of Racine's strong antitheses, pivoting round the word *dernière*. Is this a total disclaimer of responsibility, or a clearsighted recognition of her position? The formal effect once again focuses the expressive intensity and the structural point.

The tempo of this concertante passage quickens to another climax. Oenone has at last seen where Phèdre is leading her : to a confession of love. She now presses all her enquiry to a point : she stabs hard three times : in three syllables (43), two syllables (44) : one (46). Phèdre's answers are a paroxysm of broken phrases : the alexandrine melts in her anguish. At Oenone's last stab, *Qui?*, Phèdre's line goes legato, and one can almost hear a chromaticism as her will loosens, and she releases the touching periphrasis (46–47) in which she avoids mentioning the name, but indicates her love, her pride (*Ce prince ...*), another dynastic motive (*ce fils de l'Amazone*, which hints at the huntsman, and his fierce virginity), her shame (*par moi-même opprimé*).

Oenone's formal, operatic exclamation gives her the top note. The name comes flying out at last. This hemistich, and Phèdre's gently ironic balancing reply (48) formally match the equivalent line 30; another perfect cadence. So the marvellously conducted interchange of the last twenty lines has been enclosed within these symmetrically balanced figures, in a great period. And after the agitated exchange of 43–47, when phrases were tossed out in a mounting passage which broke down the structure of the metrical unit, 48 returns us to the alexandrine.

The scene continues with four lines in which Oenone's music changes: she is now desperately agitated, and tosses out a number of motives. Above that supporting but rather choppy movement Phèdre, at last, floats her great aria, beginning deep down in her register with *Mon mal vient de plus loin* . . . , and reaching a first climax with

O comble de misère !
Mes yeux le retrouvaient dans les traits de son père.

Then there is a second tremendous climax, crucially thematic, for four themes coalesce : Vénus becomes a predatory beast; Phèdre's *mal* is imagined as bursting out; her *sang* is shed; and the beast, scenting it, fixes itself on her in

C'est Vénus toute entière à sa proie attachée.

The speech winds down again from this point and breathes itself out, literally, in

Un reste de chaleur tout prêt à s'exhaler.

The voice falls away, the scene ends. The sympathetic spectator, listening to Phèdre, has reached a vicarious expiry. Then, with a tremendous twist of the plot, Racine brings on the minor character Panope, who announces, with extraordinary flatness (the driest of recitatives) the death of Thésée. The situation is overturned.

It is hard to image any operatic music before Mozart, and after him only Verdi's and Wagner's, which is equal in subtlety to this music. It is partly a matter of the flexibility of the medium, the verse; much more a matter of the intensity with which the situation is envisaged and the startling coolness with which nonetheless, every touch is planned and placed. The passage above was one of the grand moments of the play. Here by contrast is a minor passage, which shows nonetheless that the staple of this dramatic verse has the same richness of texture as the high points.

It is the conclusion of the exchange, in II ii, between Hippolyte and Aricie. Hippolyte has been betrayed by his own turbulent impulses into a confession of his love—a love he had wanted to think he was immune to—and now he wonders at his strange state. The pattern of this impulse is one of the great simple patterns of the play; immediately afterwards, Phèdre is unable to resist the impulse to declare *her* love for *him*; much later, Thésée is unable to resist the impulse to curse him. The speech begins, wonderingly and a little bitterly,

> Je me suis engagé trop avant.
> Je vois que la raison cède à la violence.

That is a theme—a moral—of the play; but I overleap a number of lines to show the delicacy with which a number of motives, subservient to the large themes, play under the surface of the verse; being heard mainly as harmonics, or reverberations, or touches of orchestration which complicate the tonality. These are the lines :

Asservi maintenant sous la commune loi,	1
Par quel trouble me vois-je emporté loin de moi ?	
Un moment a vaincu mon audace imprudente :	
Cette âme si superbe est enfin dépendante.	
Depuis près de six mois, honteux, désespéré,	5
Portant partout le trait dont je suis déchiré,	
Contre vous, contre moi, vainement je m'éprouve :	
Présente, je vous fuis; absente, je vous trouve;	
Dans le fond des forêts votre image me suit;	
La lumière du jour, les ombres de la nuit,	10
Tout retrace à mes yeux les charmes que j'évite;	
Tout vous livre à l'envi le rebelle Hippolyte.	
Moi-même, pour tout fruit de mes soins superflus,	
Maintenant je me cherche, et ne me trouve plus.	
Mon arc, mes javelots, mon char, tout m'importune;	15
Je ne me souviens plus des leçons de Neptune;	
Mes seuls gémissements font retentir les bois,	
Et mes coursiers oisifs ont oublié ma voix.	
Peut-être le récit d'un amour si sauvage	
Vous fait en m'écoutant rougir de votre ouvrage.	20

D'un coeur qui s'offre à vous quel farouche entretien !
Quel étrange captif pour un si beau lien !
Mais l'offrande à vos yeux en doit être plus chère.
Songez que je vous parle une langue étrangère,
Et ne rejetez pas des voeux mal exprimés,   25
Qu'Hippolyte sans vous n'aurait jamais formés.

Hippolyte had thought to sit on the shore, heart-whole, and watch
the shipwreck of all the lovers of the world, but he has been swept
away to slavery by the universal wave; it is a tyranny, and a disturbance which disintegrates the personality. These are two themes of
the play. Line 3, about the *coup de foudre*, echoes more soberly what
Phèdre had said in ecstasy in I iv (*Je le vis; je rougis, je pâlis à sa
vue* : an instant fever). Compare also what Aricie had said at the
beginning of this very scene : she had scorned Thésée's decree that
she should remain unmarried, because she scorned all men; but
Mes yeux alors, mes yeux n'avaient pas vu son fils.

With line 5 we reach a delicate net of imagery. Hippolyte speaks
of himself through the suppressed metaphor of a stricken deer. It is
not just Cupid's arrow in the conventional Petrarchan mode; it is a
real arrow he imagines, and he is a hunted beast. That is one theme;
is the huntress Vénus? Line 7, with its butting repetition, makes the
wound feel genuine; it conveys the movement of the deer pushing at
hedge, at tree, to remove the arrow. This makes the wound worse;
hence *déchiré* in line 6. In line 9, the reverberant phrase about the
forest echoes the other forest-motives in the play. The alternation of
La lumière du jour, les ombres de la nuit is also reminiscent of words
of Oenone's. After years of jealously building up a special identity,
Hippolyte finds that it has vanished (14) : he is lost to himself in a
sense which implies, again, that love is a psychic disturbance (cf. 2).
Lines 14–17 are deeply thematic; they link with the image of himself
as a stricken deer, and carry on that theme; and there are even more
striking echoes earlier and later in the play.

He turns back to Aricie after these lines spent ruefully assessing
his strange and unwelcome state. He is now a little anxious that he
may have made himself seem ridiculous by his frankness, his discom-
posure, his sense that he is just a boy out of his depth in his first
love (19–20). Is she ashamed of her prize, her capture? In 22 the
stricken deer has, in the word *lien*, been turned into something else.
There is a link backwards with *asservi* in 1; and with the deer : he

194

is a captive wild creature, incongruously led in a triumph. He abases himself a little, makes himself seem rustic, simple, even outlandish, as if by mocking himself to take the sting out of the mockery he fears from her.

But then something else happens. The captive creature, first hunted and wounded, then paraded, has in 23 become an *offrande*, a sacrifice. So in two words, *lien* and *offrande*, the image is almost inaudibly converted into something in tune with the hideous comment on love which the whole play is. We hardly notice it, except as a glint of savagery in the orchestration.

But it can be brought out into the open if we pursue this net of correspondences and transmutations backwards and forwards into the rest of the play. If we feel along the links, they turn out to be a steely armature which gives the play one whole element of its structure. For instance, the reference to Hippolyte's prowess as huntsman (15–16) goes back to the first scene of the play, where Théramène says (and it is already ominous):

> Avouez-le, tout change; et depuis quelques jours
> On vous voit moins souvent, orgueilleux et sauvage,

(and there is the 'wild' theme)

> Tantôt faire voler un char sur le rivage

(and there is the image of Phèdre's momentary longing in I iii)

> Tantôt, savant dans l'art par Neptune inventé,
> Rendre docile au frein un coursier indompté.
> Les forêts de nos cris moins souvent retentissent.
> Chargés d'un feu secret, vos yeux s'appesantissent.

The last line is the most intense, tonally, of the whole first scene. We have modulated from the freedom and innocence of the forest, and Hippolyte's wildness (as of the animals he hunts or tames) to the sense that *he* is hunted and tamed, and is stricken by the fever, the *mal*, of love. *Chargés* leads into *s'appesantissent*: he bears an incubus-load.

In the last scene of the play, Hippolyte is killed, under Neptune's influence, by those very horses, and there is a powerful echo backwards to these two scenes, as Théramène reports his death:

> La frayeur les emporte; et sourds à cette fois,
> Ils ne connaissent plus ni le frein ni la voix.

Phèdre's 'momentary longing', mentioned above, came out as :

> Dieux ! Que ne suis-je assise à l'ombre des forêts !
> Quant pourrai-je, au travers d'une noble poussière,
> Suivre de l'oeil un char fuyant dans la carrière !

This was her first slip, which Oenone did not notice. *Noble* means, for Phèdre, 'princely'. It is an underthought, a sad one, that the chariot, *fuyant*, is eluding her. The forest shade is perhaps for her associated with escape—escape from life itself, but to happiness, youth, freedom and simplicity. It is a very complex figure, made more so as the play goes on.

A few lines after that sigh, Oenone had pointed out that

> Les ombres par trois fois ont obscurci les cieux
> Depuis que le sommeil n'est entré dans vos yeux,
> Et le jour a trois fois chassé la nuit obscure
> Depuis que votre corps languit sans nourriture.

These solemn lines with their ritual repetition (*trois fois* suggesting a magical conjuration as in *Macbeth*), and the sense of fevered alternation, link with Hippolyte's line 10 in our passage. This again is the theme of love as consuming sickness, but it is complicated by the notion (in Phèdre's words) of a necromantic ritual, of belonging to the night.

That is confirmed, I think, in Phèdre's great confession to Oenone, just after the passage I analysed. There again we find the *coup de foudre* theme (*Je le vis; je rougis, je pâlis . . .*), also the Vénus theme, which fuses with the hunting theme and the wild beast theme and the *mal*. At the crisis of the speech, her *mal*, the fever, which rages in the blood (*sang*, which is also her tainted heredity), bursts out of her wound (cf Hippolyte's line 6); this is the scent which Venus picks up; metamorphosed into a tiger, the goddess fixes herself on the stricken deer (like Hippolyte's incubus) :

> Ma blessure trop vive aussitôt a saigné.
> Ce n'est plus une ardeur dans mes veines cachée,
> C'est Vénus toute entière à sa proie attachée.

It is a wonderful chordal passage, with the themes coalescing.

The predator is seen both as the goddess and the loved one. Both Aricie and Phèdre speak of Hippolyte as a fierce or proud young animal who must be tamed. The implication is that if he is *not* tamed, he may attack. (There is an undertone in the whole play that the loved one may have to be killed; here the theme links with the 'monster' theme and the Cretan 'labyrinth' theme naturally associated with the family of Thésée; what is found at the end of the maze must kill or be killed; and nearly everybody in the play is explicitly described, at some crucial point, as a monster). Aricie lets slip the word *dompter* in talking to Ismène of Hippolyte. Phèdre brings the notion out into the open when, having learnt at last that Hippolyte loves Aricie, she abandons herself to rage and jealousy in which values and facts are madly inverted :

> Ce farouche ennemi qu'on ne pouvait dompter,
> Qu'offensait le respect, qu'importunait la plainte,
> Ce tigre que jamais je n'abordai sans crainte,
> Soumis, apprivoisé, reconnaît un vainqueur !
> Aricie a trouvé le chemin de son coeur.

(The *chemin* is of course the way through the labyrinth.)

Hence part of the force (to return to Hippolyte's speech) of the reference to the *offrande*. Is he going to be sacrificed? There is yet another link, with Phèdre's confession to Oenone, where she had re-counted her own desperate sacrifices to the beast-goddess Vénus :

> Je lui bâtis un temple et pris soin de l'orner;
> De victimes moi-même à toute heure entourée,
> Je cherchais dans leurs flancs ma raison égarée.

There Phèdre appears as frenzied sorceress again; the rites of the religion are bestial and cruel. As she says,

> J'adorais Hippolyte; et le voyant sans cesse,
> Même au pied des autels que je faisais fumer,
> J'offrais tout à ce dieu que je n'osais nommer.

A final transformation : the loved one can be both sacrifice and god.

One could pursue these links indefinitely, so subtle and far-reaching are the correspondences : one would simply quote the whole play (singing it, so to speak, to bring out the harmonies). I must content myself with a last one : the final metamorphosis of the forest-hunting image. Just after Phèdre's lines about Hippolyte the tiger, quoted above, this nexus of images modulates from the darkness of the forest to the contrasting dominant image of sunlight, which for one moment becomes kindly. The movement is from guilt to innocence, constriction to openness, minor to major. Phèdre begins, hideously,

> De leur furtive ardeur ne pouvais-tu m'instruire?

But the note changes :

> Les a-t-on vu souvent se parler, se chercher?
> Dans le fond des forêts allaient-ils se cacher?

It has become colloquy, searching, flight. The forest brings thoughts of retreat from the light, of healing calm, the innocence of the young people, perhaps a sexuality which is itself innocent. Identifying herself in imagination with this impossible fulfilment, Phèdre's lines become free from envy as she imagines a love which is easy, approved, returned. The light floods in :

> Hélas! Ils se voyaient avec pleine licence.
> Le ciel de leurs soupirs approuvaient l'innocence;
> Ils suivaient sans remords leur penchant amoureux,
> Tous les jours se levaient clairs et sereins pour eux.

Only the elegiac note, *Hélas!*, prevents this being a rapturous dream of happiness. The imagination of this state of grace lies behind Phèdre's very last words, where she turns the final facet of the master-image, the light image, to the spectator :

> Et la mort, à mes yeux dérobant la clarté,
> Rend au jour, qu'ils souillaient, toute sa pureté.

For her it is an impossible ideal; she is an irremediable pollution.

What play has a more deeply considered melodic line or thematic structure (its *real* structure, not the imposed superstructure of 'structuralism')? It is not the rich Elizabethan surface texture that the English reader enjoys, full of rugosities and bright colours; but sober, elegant, discreet—so quiet in tone that the figures work almost at the level of cliché. They are live, however, and to enter the structure at any point, to listen and to feel what is going on is to catch these dismaying sonorities.

A passage quoted by Professor Vinaver in his *Racine and Poetic Tragedy* runs :

> 'M. Racine,' says the unknown chronicler, 'had by nature a talent for reciting verses in the most natural and persuasive way.

198

. . . He did not approve of the too even manner of reciting established in Molière's company. He wanted verse to be given a certain sound which, joined to the measure and the rhymes, would distinguish it from prose; but he could not endure those extravagant yelping sounds which people wanted to substitute for perfect naturalness and which could, so to speak, be given notes like music. Shocked by this bad taste which was beginning to appear, he arrived one day to find the players assembled. "Gentlemen," he said to them, "I bring you some bad news. Your theatre is going to be closed." "For what reason, Sir?" said one of them. "For what reason?" replied M. Racine. "You should know that Lully alone has leave to make actors sing in this theatre, and it appears that quite inappropriately you sing in yours." '

This anecdote indicates once more the limitations of the analogy. Racine, I am convinced, saw the relationship with music : but like other poets at other times he was interested in recovering for verse *son bien*, in danger of being appropriated by music. The point is expressed by saying that dramatic verse at its highest compels the analogy, but it needs no music which it has not itself provided.

Index

DATE DUE